Islamic Commercial Law

Founded in 1807, John Wiley & Sons is the oldest independent publishing company in the United States. With offices in North America, Europe, Australia, and Asia, Wiley is globally committed to developing and marketing print and electronic products and services for our customers' professional and personal knowledge and understanding.

The Wiley Finance series contains books written specifically for finance and investment professionals as well as sophisticated individual investors and their financial advisors. Book topics range from portfolio management to e-commerce, risk management, financial engineering, valuation, and financial instrument analysis, as well as much more.

For a list of available titles, please visit our website at www.WileyFinance.com.

Islamic Commercial Law

Muhammad Yusuf Saleem

WILEY

John Wiley & Sons Singapore Pte. Ltd.

Published by John Wiley & Sons Singapore Pte. Ltd., 1 Fusionopolis Walk, #07-01, Solaris South Tower, Singapore 138628

Other Wiley Editorial Offices
John Wiley & Sons, 111 River Street, Hoboken, NJ 07030, USA
John Wiley & Sons, The Atrium, Southern Gate, Chichester, West Sussex, P019 8SQ, United Kingdom
John Wiley & Sons (Canada) Ltd., 5353 Dundas Street West, Suite 400, Toronto, Ontario, M9B 6HB, Canada
John Wiley & Sons Australia Ltd., 42 McDougall Street, Milton, Queensland 4064, Australia
Wiley-VCH, Boschstrasse 12, D-69469 Weinheim, Germany

ISBN 978-1-118-50403-1 (Paperback)
ISBN 978-1-118-50404-8 (ePDF)
ISBN 978-1-118-50405-5 (Mobi)
ISBN 978-1-118-50406-2 (ePub)

Typeset in 11/14pt, Arno Pro by MPS Limited, Chennai, India.
Printed in Singapore by Markono Print Media.

10 9 8 7 6 5 4 3 2 1

In the Name of God, the Merciful, the
Compassionate

Praise be to God, Lord of the Universes,
The Gracious, the Merciful,
Master of the Day of Judgement.

You alone we worship; You alone we implore for help.

Guide us unto the straight path—
The path of those whom You have blessed,
Those who have not incurred Your displeasure,
Those who have not gone astray.

Amen
Qur'an, 1: 1–7

Contents

Preface

Islamic commercial law is an important component of *al-fiqhal-mu'amalat.* Its fundamental principles are provided by the *Qur'an* and the *Sunnah.* In the light of these principles, Muslim jurists have provided in great detail scholarly works on each individual contract. Islamic contracts are seen as a means that provide various options in order to obtain permissible (*halal*) earnings. Earning in a permissible way is considered an act of worship (*'ibadah*) in Islam. Muslim jurists in their voluminous books on Islamic *Fiqh* have discussed together the rules pertaining to worship (*fiqh al-'ibadat*) and the rules pertaining to commerce and business (*fiqh al-mu'amalat*) and give them equal treatment and significance. A chapter would discuss the pillars (*arkan*) and conditions (*shurut*) for prayer (*salat*), while the next chapter would discuss the pillars and conditions of sale (*bay'*) or partnership (*musharakah*) contracts. Any discussion on a certain contract would take into account the prohibitions of usury (*riba*), ambiguity (*gharar*), gambling (*maysir*), and other unlawful practises. The holistic approach adopted by Muslim jurists would also relate discussions on an individual contract to the objectives of *Shari'ah,* which further supplemented the already existing body of literature on Islamic commercial and financial laws.

Islamic banking and finance is contract-based banking and finance. An Islamic bank has to establish *Shari'ah*-compliant contractual relationship with its customers both on deposit and financing sides. Various Islamic contracts are also used in different *sukuk* structures for raising funds and their subsequent use. The knowledge of Islamic contracts is therefore central to any commercial, business, and banking activity. Thus, there is a renewed and growing interest in the study of Islamic contracts. However, there is also an increasing tendency among both students and practitioners of Islamic banking and finance to study individual contracts and transactions without referring to their philosophical foundations and the objectives of *Shari'ah.* There is a danger that there would be a greater emphasis on procedural and legal formalities of contracts while their substance and the purposes for which they are intended may largely be ignored. This would be a departure from the holistic approach that characterised Islamic law of transactions for centuries.

Each individual contract has its own pillars and conditions. Pillars (*rukun*, plural *arkan*) refer to the main constituent element of a contract without which a contract is not complete. Generally, pillars of a contract include the parties to a contract, the subject matter of a contract, and the offer and acceptance (which show the mutual consent of the parties). There are also conditions for each pillar of a contract—for instance, conditions related to the parties to have the requisite legal capacity (*ahliyyah*), conditions related to the object of the contract to be well defined and known, or conditions related to the language of an offer and acceptance to be clear. Conditions in a contract are meant to avoid ambiguities (*gharar*), usury (*riba*), gambling (*maysir*), and other prohibited elements. One of the important functions of conditions is to protect both parties and to manage possible risk that may arise from the contract. We have discussed the pillars for each individual contract and its important conditions. Since conditions related to the legal capacity of the contracting parties are universally applicable to all contracts, in this book unless necessary I have not repeated them for each individual contract. The assumption is that the parties to a contract have the requisite legal capacity. Instead the focus is on other conditions that are unique to that individual contract.

This book developed during my years of teaching at the *Kulliyyah* of Economics and Management Sciences, International Islamic University Malaysia. I was motivated to write this book primarily by the shortage of English books on Islamic commercial and financial transactions that would combine the theory with the practise. There was a need for a textbook that would discuss Islamic contracts with a view to practise them and to avoid discussions on detailed issues that fill volumes in the available works of *Fiqh*. At the same time, the book should not only discuss the form of individual transactions but also their substance and purposes. This book begins with an introductory discussion on the prohibited practises. The first two chapters discuss the contract of sale and its various types. In the succeeding chapters other contracts are discussed. A chapter is devoted to a discussion on an individual contract. However, in certain chapters two or three contracts are combined due to their similarities. The book also uses diagrams to explain contractual relationships between the parties and where necessary discusses their applications. At the end of each chapter, true/false and short answer questions are provided to enable readers to evaluate their understanding of the various contracts. Answers to the true/false questions can be found at the end of the book. For the sake of accuracy and convenience I have provided both the Arabic origin and the English translations of the *Qur'anic* verses and *ahadith* (singular *hadith*).

I take this opportunity to express my gratefulness to Allah (swt) for granting me the ability, health, and patience to complete this work.

Muhammad Yusuf Saleem
International Islamic University Malaysia
Kuala Lumpur
Ramadhan 1433
July, 2012

List of Abbreviations

Abbreviations

swt	*Subhanahuwata'ala*
pbAbuh	Peace and blessing of Allah be upon him.
mAbpwh	May Allah be pleased with him/her.
mAbpwt	May Allah be pleased with them.

Acknowledgments

I take this opportunity to thank the IIUM Institute of Islamic Banking and Finance (II*i*BF), who asked me to produce a textbook on Islamic commercial law. In particular, I acknowledge the support I have received from Prof. Datuk Dr. Mohd Azmi Omar, the former Dean of II*i*BF and the current Director General of Islamic Research and Training Institute (IRTI), Jeddah, Saudi Arabia. Thanks are also due to Prof. Dr. Khaliq Ahmad, Dean *Kulliyyah* of Economics and Management Sciences and my colleagues at the Department of Economics and the *Kulliyyah* of Economics and Management Sciences, International Islamic University Malaysia for their encouragement and support. I would also like to thank Emilie Herman, Senior Editorial Manager, and Stefan Skeen, Senior Production Editor at John Wiley & Sons, and the rest of the editorial staff for their helpful suggestions that added clarity to the book. This book benefitted a great deal from the classroom discussions that I have had with my students at both the graduate and undergraduate levels over the years. Without their contributions and invaluable suggestions this book would have been incomplete. A work of this nature involves references to the primary sources of *Fiqh*, which are the *Qur'an* and the *Sunnah*, and the secondary sources, which are the voluminous *Fiqh* books written by jurists of different *Fiqh* schools. These references are necessary in order to ensure that an opinion or a ruling is accurately attributed to a particular jurist or *Fiqh* school. I would like to acknowledge that I have benefitted from Dr. Wahbah al-Zuhaili's *Financial Transactions in Islamic Jurisprudence* as translated by Mahmoud A. El-Gamal and Sayyid Saabiq's *Fiqh al-Sunnah*. The author, however, is solely responsible for any errors which may be found in the book or for the views expressed.

Introduction

An Overview of Prohibited Elements

The *Qur'an* and the *Sunnah* are the two main sources of Islamic commercial laws. It was revealed at a time when both Makkah and Medina were blooming commercial centers of Arabia. The *Qur'an* and the *Sunnah* did not totally abolish the pre-Islamic commercial practices. They approved all those transactions that did not conflict with the principles of *Shari'ah*; corrected and modified some other transactions by eliminating unjust and prohibited elements from them; and prohibited some other business practices that had usurious elements, or suffered from *gharar*, and fraud. This approach towards commercial and business practices is characterised by its focus on the prohibition of specific practices rather than on the enumeration of permissible transactions. The approach led the Muslim jurists to conclude that in commercial transactions (*mu'amalat*) the principle is permissibility, whereas prohibition is an exception. Hence, every commercial transaction that is not specifically prohibited or does not contain prohibited elements is permissible. This has facilitated the adoption of commercial transactions that are customarily practised by the people and that do not go against the *Shari'ah* prohibitions. It also encourages innovation and creativity when new *Shari'ah*-compliant products could be engineered. This is in stark contrast to matters of worship (*'ibadat*), in which any innovation is considered heresy (*bid'ah*). The main practices that are prohibited are usury, ambiguity in contracts (*gharar*), gambling and games of chance (*maysir*), fraud, bribery, the use of false weights and measures, taking others' property unlawfully, and transactions on prohibited (*haram*) things.

Usury (*Riba*)

The *Qur'an* and the *ahadith* have forbidden usury (*riba*) in the strongest terms. The *Qur'an* has warned that those who practise usury are at war with God and His Apostle. The word *riba* denotes increase, addition, or excess. *Riba* refers to a stipulated increase over and above the loan amount that a debtor agrees to pay to his creditor in relation to a specific period of time. Charging an extra amount for the time, irrespective of the outcome of the enterprise, is considered injustice. The borrowed money would have to be invested and combined with efforts, and there could be the possibilities of profit and loss. The shares of fund owner and fund user should be tied and connected to the underlying economic activities. They are entitled to receive a certain predetermined percentage of the actual profit made by the investments. A fund provider cannot claim a certain fixed rate of interest irrespective of the performance of the investment. Islamic law, therefore, recommends profit-and-loss-sharing contracts. In contrast, in usury the return to the usurer is fixed in advance. The usurer is guaranteed a certain cost for his fund irrespective of the actual outcome from the investment. This predetermination of return to the usurer ignores the economic realities on the ground and, therefore, introduces distortion into the market, particularly when we consider that the predetermined interest is added to the cost of production and the prices of goods.

Moreover, it is one of the objectives of *Shari'ah* that wealth should benefit not only its owner, but also the other contracting party and the society as a whole. This is best achieved when the risks and rewards of investment are shared between the fund owner and its user. In contrast, usury only guarantees a certain predetermined rate of return to the fund owner and ignores its user. A needy person who borrows money for consumption purposes is required to pay back more than what he has borrowed, and a person who borrows capital for trade and business has to take the risk of loss in case the business fails. The capital provider is guaranteed his capital plus interest and protected from losses. The risks of investments are entirely shifted to the borrowers.

Some writers have differentiated between usury and interest on the ground that the former involves loans for consumption, whereas the latter involves loans for production. Interest, they argue, is an extra charge imposed on a debtor who borrows money for productive purposes such as investment, industry, and trade, whereas usury is an extra charge imposed on a debtor who borrows money for consumption such as his own personal day-to-day needs. They argue that interest is a reasonable charge for the use of money employed in productive purposes, whereas usury is unjust and forbidden. This view, however, could not be maintained. A debtor who borrows money for investment, trade, and business may face one of four possible situations: He may make enough profit to pay the capital and interest and keep the balance. Second, it is also possible that he may make profit enough to pay for the interest, whereas he may not get any share of the profit. Third, there is the possibility that he may not earn any profit, in which case he has to return the principal and pay the interest. Fourth, he may suffer losses. In these three out of four possible scenarios, the transaction is not fair to the borrower. Even in the first example, the transaction is not fair to the lender, as it is possible that the borrower may keep a larger share of the profit for himself and return a smaller percentage to him. Thus, charging interest on loans granted for productive purposes could also be exploitative and unjust to either or both of the parties. It is therefore argued that *riba* covers all types of loans in which interest is charged, regardless of whether they are made for consumption or production purposes.

Ambiguities in a Contract (*Gharar*)

The other prohibited practice is *gharar,* which enables a person to obtain another's property unlawfully and may subsequently lead to disputes and disagreements between them. *Gharar* literally means "uncertainty," "ambiguity," "danger," or "peril." Technically *bay al-gharar* refers to a sale contract that is attractive to the purchaser in its form but unknown and ambiguous in its substance. It also refers to ambiguity in a sale contract that may lead to unknown results. The *Sunnah* of the Prophet (pbAbuh) has specifically prohibited transactions that involved elements of *gharar.* These include sale transactions concluded by throwing stones, by mere touching without proper inspection, or by chance.

The main reason for the prohibition of *gharar* is the existence of vagueness in rights and liabilities that can be exploited to deceive people into thinking that they are getting a better deal, which, in reality, is not the case. More frequently, such ambiguities in a certain contract are designed to commit fraud and cheat one of the parties. Ambiguity in a certain contract may arise when its pillars and conditions are not clearly defined. A sale contract in which information concerning the subject matter, the price, or the parties is not disclosed suffers from ambiguity (*gharar*). Selling goods without specifying their prices, such as selling at the market price and selling goods without proper description or without allowing the buyer to properly examine the goods, are examples of transactions that involve *gharar. Gharar* also exists when a certain product is sold without label. A label usually states the contents of the product and its expiry date. The absence of proper labeling means that the subject matter of the sale is not clearly defined. Label is particularly crucial for nondurable items such as fish, meat, dairy products, and medicines. Without labels, the items cannot be clearly known and consumers are made to pay without supplying them with sufficient information. *Gharar* also exists in a sale of houses under construction where the quality of construction materials or the time for the completion of the houses and their delivery date is not known. *Gharar* also exists when a developer is free to change the specifications of the house, its interior or exterior design, with or without prior notice. Similarly, *gharar* may also exist in a sale of new vehicles when the time of delivery is not certain, which may result in several postponements of the delivery, or when last minute changes are made to the color, scheme, or other specifications. A deferred sale may involve *gharar* if the term of the payment is not known—for instance, when the number of installments, the duration of installments, or the mode of payment is not clearly defined. Selling some products without disclosing their side effects and other crucial information involves *gharar.* The side effects of such products are sometimes detrimental to health and may cause other life-threatening problems. This also amounts to cheating. Had the information been fully disclosed, the buyer might not have purchased them.

Such contracts are therefore considered void on the grounds of *gharar* because the ambiguities they contain may cause harm to one of the parties and unjustified enrichment to the other.

In order to eliminate the possibilities of *gharar,* Muslim jurists have laid down various conditions for different contracts. Generally, in a certain contract, all conditions concerning offer and acceptance, the parties, the price, and the subject matter should be fulfilled. For instance, in order to prevent *gharar,* the quality and quantity of the subject matter, its price, the date of payment if the payment is deferred, the date of delivery, and any other pertinent and necessary details of the contract must be clearly defined.

If the existence of *gharar* invalidates a sale contract, it can also invalidate other contracts. It is therefore possible to extend the concept of *gharar* to other contracts when their pillars and conditions are not well defined. For instance, a contract of employment (*ijarah*) suffers from *gharar* when the rights and duties of the employer and employee are not clearly defined. Similarly, *gharar* also exists if an investor provides capital to another without specifying the nature of the relationship that exists between them and other relevant details, such as the percentage of profit or loss sharing.

Gharar is distinguished from risk that is naturally associated with certain business ventures concerning the possibilities of loss or profit. Risk refers to uncertainties about the expected profit or the occurrence of a loss. *Gharar* refers to a potentially deceptive ambiguity in a certain contract, whereas risk is a type of uncertainty that is not designed to cheat and does not lead to disputes between the parties. *Gharar* arises when relevant information in a contract is not disclosed, whereas risk exists even when there is a full disclosure of information. For instance, manufacturers, importers, exporters, and traders are uncertain whether their products and goods could find a suitable market. They are uncertain about the amount of profit and the possibility of loss. This type of uncertainty is neither intentionally created by the parties nor designed to commit fraud. The parties make all the efforts to minimise losses. However, they cannot totally eliminate the possibilities of loss and guarantee profit. This type of risk is combined with efforts that may eventually lead to profit.

Gambling (*Maysir*)

Maysir literally means a way of easily obtaining something without any effort. The term *maysir* applies to all activities in which a person wins or loses by mere chance. It includes all kinds of gambling. In gambling, the winner and the loser win or lose by mere chance. The winner does not lawfully earn what he has won, and the loser loses his money without a fair compensation. Gambling also covers betting on horseracing, soccer matches, and lotteries. Gambling allows the winner to consume others' property unlawfully and unjustly because in gambling there is no exchange of countervalues between the parties. Consequently, it gives rise to hostility, hatred, and enmity between the winners and the losers. It is for these reasons that all agreements and contracts that involve elements of chance (*maysir*) are prohibited. Islam encourages people to earn their living through honest effort and prohibits appropriating others' property by chance.

Prohibited (*Haram*) Properties

The property on which a certain contract is concluded should be permissible (*halal*). A contract that involves a prohibited property is void. For example, contracts involving wine, intoxicants, pigs, blood, idols, crosses, and statues are not valid because Muslims are prohibited to do business in forbidden things. Any earnings from such business are sinful. Muslims are prohibited to own, use, produce, manufacturer, import, or export prohibited (*haram*) goods or goods that contain *haram* elements. Prohibiting the sale of *haram* things to a great extent prevents people from indulging in them, whereas permitting their sale amounts to their promotion and propagation among Muslims. The implication of this prohibition for the Muslims is to come up with alternative *halal* industries and products that would substitute the *haram* ones.

A person should not use his wealth to corrupt others by investing his wealth in prohibited ventures such as gambling casinos, pornography, or in the promotion of other forbidden (*haram*) activities. It is prohibited for a Muslim to become a shareholder in a company that indulges in prohibited activities. If the primary activity of a company is based on *riba*, gambling (*maysir*), ambiguities (*gharar*), and the production and sale of prohibited goods, then it is also prohibited to sell and purchase the shares of those companies. For instance, it is not permitted for a Muslim to purchase the shares of conventional banks; companies that run casinos and gambling; companies that process, produce, and market alcoholic beverages or supply non-*halal* meat like pork; or companies that provide immoral services like prostitution, pubs, and discos.

CHAPTER

1

The Contract of Sale (*Bay'*)

Learning outcomes

At the end of this chapter, you should be able to:

1. Define a sale contract and identify its main constituent elements and important conditions.
2. Explain the differences between the subject matter of a sale and its price and the consequences of this difference.
3. Demonstrate knowledge of valid and void conditions.
4. Distinguish a sale contract from a promise to sell and identify prohibited sales and practising.
5. Explain issues related to price determination.
6. Understand and explain the juristic opinions on the contentious contracts of *bay' al-urbun*, *bay' al-dayn*, *bay' al-'einah*, and *tawarruq*.

Introduction

Islam allows the parties the freedom to exchange or sell and purchase their properties and services. It only stipulates that people should not take each other's property in an unfair (*batil*) way. Fairness is a dominant issue in exchange/sale of properties. Unfair (*batil*) ways include usury, gambling, ambiguities in agreements that can be exploited by the parties, fraud, false measurement, bribery, and theft. Exchanges of properties, if done properly, could become tools for the redistribution of wealth in a society. The *Qur'an* commands that properties should be exchanged through trade (*tijarah*) and with mutual consent (*tarad*). It states: "O ye who believe! Do not devour your property among yourselves unlawfully, but let there be among you trade by mutual consent."[1]

يَا أَيُّهَا الَّذِينَ آمَنُواْ لاَ تَأْكُلُواْ أَمْوَالَكُمْ بَيْنَكُمْ بِالْبَاطِلِ إِلاَّ أَن تَكُونَ تِجَارَةً عَن تَرَاضٍ مِّنكُمْ

The Arabic word for sale is *Bay'*, which literally means exchange (*mubadalah*) and applies to both sale and purchase. Legally, sale is defined as an exchange of a property for another, one of which is called the object, and the other the price. Sale can also be defined as an acquisition of ownership over a property in return for a consideration or compensation (*'iwad*). Sale (*Bay'*) is the most extensively used contract in the market. It covers activities ranging from the ordinary day-to-day sale and purchase of necessities to the sale of shares in the stock market and international trade among nations. Advanced and complicated entities such as a company, a firm, a partnership (*musharakah*), a *mudarabah*, and multinational companies are formed in order to sell and purchase goods, commodities, or services. Nations sell and purchase through imports and exports. In contrast to sale, all other transactions take secondary positions. The significance of a sale contract could be understood from the fact that, unlike other contracts, the *Qur'an* specifically refers to it. The *Qur'an* states: "But Allah has permitted trade (*bay'*) and forbidden usury."[2]

وَأَحَلَّ اللَّهُ الْبَيْعَ وَحَرَّمَالرِّبَا

The Prophet (pbAbuh) is reported to have said: "The best earning is where a person earns through his own efforts and all sale transactions that are free from deception and cheating."[3]

أفضل الكسب عمل الرجل بيده و كل بيع مبرور

In another *hadith* it is stated: "Sale is constituted by mutual consent."[4]

إنما البيع عن تراض

The effect of a sale contract is to transfer the ownership of the sold property from the seller to the purchaser and the ownership of the price from the purchaser to the seller. Sale allows both the parties to use their acquired properties in any way they like within the limits of the *Shari'ah*.

The Pillars of a Sale Contract

According to the Hanafii jurists, a sale contract has two pillars: offer and acceptance. They argue that the parties to a contract and the subject matter of a contract are not the pillars but are the requirements of a sale contract. They argue that offer and acceptance show consent and necessarily include and imply the existence of the parties and the subject matter. The majority of the *Fiqh* schools, on the other hand, argue that there are three pillars to a sale contract. They are expression (*sighah*), which includes offer and acceptance, the contracting parties (*al-'aqidan*), and the subject matter (*mahal al-'aqd*) or the property on which a sale contract is concluded.

Expression in a Sale Contract

Expression includes offer and acceptance. According to the Hanafiis, the party who first expresses his willingness to make a contract is making an offer (*ijab*). The party who first expresses his consent could be a buyer or a seller. The expression of willingness coming from the other party is termed acceptance (*qabul*). In contrast, according to the majority of the *Fiqh* schools, offer is a statement that comes from the seller who, as an owner of a property, offers it for sale. The statement that comes from the buyer, according to them, amounts to acceptance. According to them, even if the first statement comes from the buyer and the second statement from the seller, the latter is considered offer and the former is acceptance.

Offer and acceptance could be expressed verbally, by acts when we buy items with a price tag in a supermarket without uttering words, by gestures such as in a stock exchange where shares are sold and purchased, or through writings. They can also be made through modern means of communications such as fax and Internet, which are considered written exchanges. Furthermore, exchange of offer and acceptance through machines that dispense food and drink, or coins, are considered to be written exchanges.

The conditions for the expression:

- The offer and acceptance must be clear and should not be ambiguous.
- The acceptance must be unconditional. It must be made to correspond with the offer. A sale contract is not valid if there is any variation between offer and acceptance. For example, there is no agreement between offer and acceptance when a seller wants to sell his goods for cash and the purchaser wants to pay by instalments for the same price or when the seller wants the price in Ringgit and the purchaser wants to pay in Euros.
- The connection between the offer and acceptance should take place in the session of a contract (*majlis al-'aqd*).[5]
- Both offer and acceptance should be made in the past or present perfect tenses.

The Parties to a Sale Contract

There should be more than one party to a sale contract. There is no sale contract when the same person acts as a buyer and a seller, except when a father, guardian, or judge sells their own property to a minor or purchases a minor's property from him.

The condition for the parties:

Both the seller and the purchaser should have complete legal capacity. A sale transaction can only be concluded by parties who have attained the age of majority and have the requisite legal capacity (*ahliyyah*). A child, a lunatic person, or a prodigal (*safih*), for instance, cannot conclude a sale contract. They are in need of guardians to act on their behalf. According to the Hanafiis, the age of majority is 18 for males and 17 for females, whereas to the other schools, it is 15 for both males and females.[6] A person who has reached the age of majority can distinguish between useful and harmful, profitable and unprofitable sale transactions. He may, therefore, decide whether to conclude a sale contract or not without an approval from the guardian.

The Subject Matter and the Price in a Sale Contract

If a person exchanges a computer for 500 kg of rice, which one is the price and which one is the subject matter or the thing sold? In order to answer this question we must first understand the definitions of the subject matter and the price. The subject matter or the thing sold (*mubee'*) is the principal object of a sale contract. It is a well-defined, particularised, and specific thing. The people purchase them in order to use and benefit from them. The price (*thaman*), on the other hand, is a medium of exchange that facilitates the acquisition of the properties. Although a price should be known and fixed, it is not a particularised or specific thing because any banknotes or coins of a certain currency may serve as a price. For example, when a specific car is sold for RM 10,000, the car is known and specified, whereas RM 10,000 could be made of any notes of any denominations. Figure 1.1 shows the sold item and the price.

A price or money (*thaman*) is a medium of exchange, a store of value, and a unit of accounting. Some properties have these attributes of money and could always be used as a price. These comprise gold coins (*dinar*) and silver coins (*dirham*) and, by analogy, all currencies. There are other types of properties that are always the thing sold and cannot be used as a price. This group comprises nonhomogeneous properties such as land, houses, trees, cars, and so forth. These properties cannot be used as prices because they cannot become units of accounting. When these properties are sold they must be specified and particularised. Some other types of properties could be used sometimes as a price and sometimes as the thing sold or the subject matter of a sale contract. This comprises all homogeneous (*mithli*) commodities that are measured, weighed, or numbered such as wheat, rice, barley, dates, salt, palm oil, fruits, and so forth. When these commodities are exchanged with *dinar, dirham,* or currencies, they are considered as the subject matters of sale or the things sold. When they are exchanged with other homogeneous

FIGURE 1.1 A person sells a specific well-defined item. The purchaser pays the price, which could be any banknotes or coins of a currency.

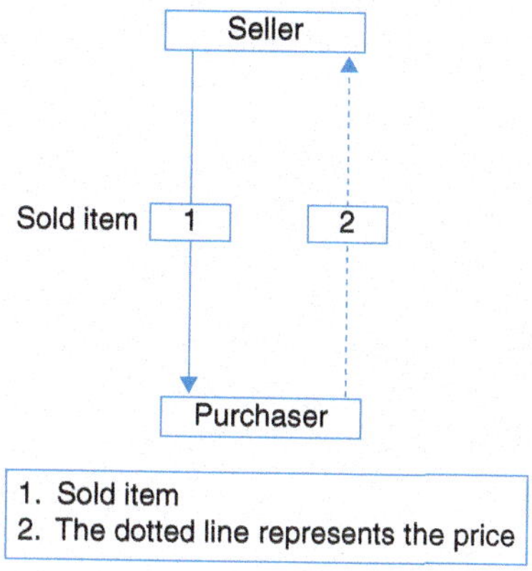

properties, if one of them is specified and particularised, it is considered as the subject matter, and the other, which is known and fixed but indeterminate, is the price. For example, a known bag of 5 kg of a specified brand of rice is sold in exchange for 10 kg of rambutan fruit. The bag of rice, which is known and specified, is the subject matter of the sale, whereas any 10 kg of *rambutan* constitutes the price.

Following are the conditions related to the subject matter of a sale contract:

- Both the subject matter and the price should be valuable properties.
- The subject matter, as distinguished from the price, should be in existence at the time of the sale. Exceptions are made with regard to *salam* and *istisna'* contracts.
- The subject matter must be deliverable or the seller should be capable of delivering the object of sale.
- The subject matter should be known to the purchaser by sight or description. If it is sold only by description, the buyer has the option to cancel the contract after seeing the object if it is not in accordance with the description. If the seller describes goods to be sold as being of a certain quality and the goods, upon inspection, prove to be of inferior quality or value, the purchaser may decide whether to cancel the sale under the option of inspection or to accept the goods.
- The price should be known to both parties. The type and quantum of the currency should be specified. If the currency is not specified, the currency that is commonly in circulation in the locality where the sale is concluded would be used. However, if in a certain place, different currencies are in circulation and the sale contract is not specific on the type of currency, the contract is voidable in accordance with the Hanafiis and depends on the approval of the parties, whereas to the majority of the *Fiqh* schools, it is void. Similarly, it is not allowed, for instance, to sell a car for the current market price and the current price is not defined. All these constitute ambiguity (*gharar*) that may lead to disputes between the parties.

FIGURE 1.2 A person cannot sell his house that he has mortgaged to another because the pledgee/mortgagee has a right in the house.

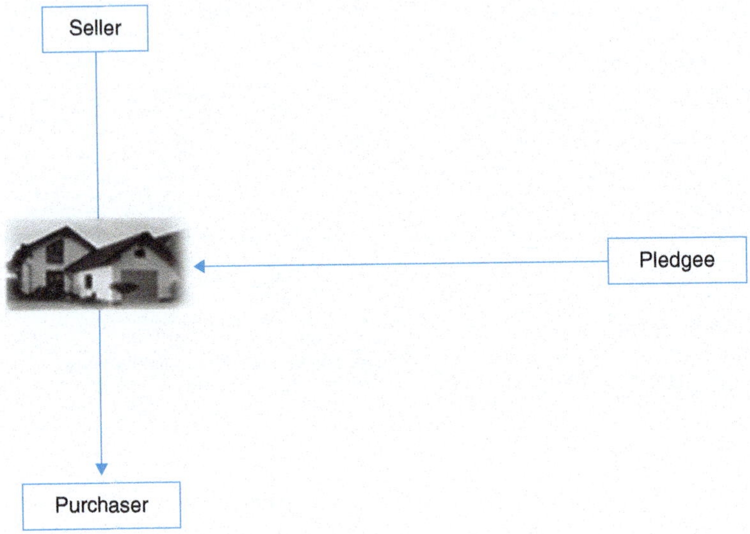

Following are the conditions for the execution of sale:

- The subject matter of sale should be owned by the seller. A sale entered into by an unauthorised agent (*fudhuli*) depends on the approval of the owner, according to Hanafiis and Malikis. The sale, however, is void according to the Shafiis and to Hanbalis who do not recognise unauthorised agency (*fudhuli*).[7]
- Third parties should have no right in the property that is offered for sale. The existence of any such right prevents the sale from being operative until the impediment is removed. For instance, a person cannot sell a house that he has already mortgaged/charged or leased, as shown in Figure 1.2. According to the Hanafiis, the contract is dependent (*mowquf*), which can only be executed after permission is given by the pledgee or the tenant. However, to the majority, the sale is void and cannot be executed.[8]

Following are the conditions for the validity of sale:

- A sale contract is not valid if the subject matter is sold for a limited time. For example, one cannot sell a house to a purchaser for only one year. If a house is sold for a year, in substance it is a lease contract and not a sale.
- A sale should be free from coercion (*ikrah*), mistake, and fraud.
- A sale should be free from vitiating or invalidating conditions. These are conditions that are not in harmony with the sale contract, that are not within the usual scope of a sale transaction, that depend on events that are imaginative, or for which the time of occurrence cannot be predicted with any degree of certainty.
- In a credit sale, the terms of payment should be known, such as the duration of instalments and the amount payable in each instalment; otherwise it is invalid.

Condition to render a sale binding:

A valid sale contract could still be cancelled if the parties and, in particular, the purchaser want to exercise his options. These can include the options of defect, conditions, and inspection. In the absence of options, a contract of sale is considered binding and cannot be cancelled, except with the mutual consent of the parties.

Conditions That May Be Put by the Parties

The parties may add conditions that are harmonious with the nature of a contract. For instance, a seller may require a down payment of the buyer in return for a stated delay in the payment of the price of the goods. Another example of such conditions is taken from the act of the Prophet (pbAbuh). Jabir bin Abdullah sold his horse to the Prophet on the condition that the horse would be delivered to him in Madinah.[9] According to the Hanafii, Shafi'i, and Maliki schools of *Fiqh*, conditions put by the parties can either be valid or void. Valid conditions are then subdivided into three categories.

- The first group includes those conditions that confirm the effects of sale. For instance, a condition in a contract of sale stipulating that the subject matter of sale should be delivered to the buyer's address is valid. This condition confirms the effect of sale that is the transfer of ownership to the purchaser. Similarly, a seller may stipulate that he shall keep the sold item until total payment is made. These conditions impose no additional obligations on either of the contracting parties.[10]
- The second category refers to those conditions the effects of which agree with the purpose of the contract of sale. For example, the seller may require pledge or a guarantor if the buyer wants to pay the price later.
- The third category includes those conditions that are customarily accepted. For example, the purchaser may require certain services that according to customs a seller should provide. These may include stipulating a guarantee period during which the purchaser may demand repairing of the sold item. The Hanafis have accepted the latter condition on the basis of *istihsan,* whereas the Shafi'is and Malikis have accepted the condition as a matter of principle. They argue that the purchaser is entitled to enjoy the use of the sold item.

Void Conditions

The *Shari'ah* prohibits all those conditions that may favour one of the parties at the expense of another or conditions that may lead to usury. The *Shari'ah* also prohibits a sale contract that comprises two agreements, one of which is a condition for the other. For example, a person is not allowed to sell an item on the condition that the purchaser sells him something else to replace it, or buys some other article, or rents him the sold property, or lends him either its price or some other sum. Similarly, it is not permitted to provide a loan on the condition that the borrower should buy a certain item from the lender. Such conditions are null and void, whether they are imposed by the seller or by the buyer.

Sale and the Promise (*Wa'ad*) to Sell

Both offer and acceptance should be made in the past or present perfect tenses. If offer and acceptance or one of them is made in the future tense, the sale contract is not valid. Making an offer to sell a certain item in the future or an acceptance to purchase it in the future is essentially a promise. Such a promise does not transfer the ownership to the purchaser. For example, "I will sell my house to you next month" and "I will purchase your house from you next month" are statements of promises that indicate that the parties have the intention to enter into a sale contract next month. This means that the parties have not entered into a sale contract yet and, as such, the ownership of the sold item is not transferred. Ownership remains with the seller and can only be transferred with mutual present consent of both parties. Thus, a promise merely amounts to an agreement to give consent in the future. Although it is strongly recommended that a promise be fulfilled (the *Qur'an*: 17:34, 61:2, 23:8), it cannot be enforced by the court of law. The court cannot force an owner to sell his property or a prospective purchaser to purchase a property on the basis of their promises. A breach of promise is, therefore, distinguished from a breach of a contract as the former falls in the realm of morality.

However, a promise is binding when it is conditional and the promise relies on the promise and fulfills the condition. For example, A promises to B that if B purchases property C he will buy it from B for a certain agreed upon price. B relies on this promise and purchases property C in order to sell it to A. A has to keep his promise and purchase the property from B, failing which A has to compensate B for the cost he has incurred for acquiring property C and for searching and reselling it to another purchaser.

Prohibited Sales and Practices

Following are examples of sale transactions that contain elements of *gharar*. These transactions could lead to unjust appropriation of other people's properties and subsequently to quarrel, conflict, and litigation and were therefore prohibited by the Prophet (pbAbuh).

Bay' al Hasat

It was a type of transaction that was conducted by throwing stones. According to this transaction, which was practice during pre-Islamic times, the vendor and the purchaser would agree that a pebble thrown to the air would decide which of the commodities would be sold. If the pebble, for example, would fall on a certain cloth, sheep, or camel, the purchaser would have to buy that particular cloth, sheep, or camel. This type of transaction involved uncertainty.

Bay' al-Mulamasah

It refers to a sale in which a piece of cloth already folded would be sold and bought merely by touching. The parties would also renounce their right of option in advance. A man would touch a garment but was not allowed to unfold or examine it.

Bay' al Munabadhah

It refers to a sale by throwing. It was a sale concluded by throwing a cloth, an article, or a pebble from one to another to signify the sale without any examination. One person would throw a garment to another, and the other would also throw a garment without either making any inspection. Each of them would say, "This is for that."

Bay' al-Muwasafah

It refers to a sale of goods that had not been possessed or inspected. The short-selling goods would only be described and its delivery would be made later.

Bay' al-Muzabanah

Muzabanah refers to a sale of exchange in which fruits of unspecified weight were sold in bulk for a definite weight, measure, or number of some other fruits—for example, an exchange of an unknown amount of green dates for a definite measure of ripe dates.

Bay' al-Mukhadarah

The farmer in pre-Islamic times would sell their fruits and vegetables or grain before they started to ripen. The practice would give rise to a lot of disputes, quarrels, and feuds because of fluctuations in the quantity and quality of these commodities or other losses that may happen. The Prophet (pbAbuh) is reported to have prohibited such a sale: "Do not purchase fruits till their quality is evident."

Bay' al-Haml

It refers to a sale of fetus or the sale of an animal to be brought forth later from the fetus of an animal. The contract implied that a she-camel would give birth and then the offspring would grow up and become pregnant. Further, one would pay the price of a she-camel that was not yet born but that would be born from the immediate offspring of an extant she-camel. The Prophet (pbAbuh) is reported to have prohibited such a contract. Narrated 'Abdullah: The people used to sell camels on the basis of Habal-al-Habala. The Prophet forbade such sale. Nafi' explained Habalal-Habala by saying, "The camel is to be delivered to the buyer after the she-camel gives birth."[11]

عَنْ عَبْدِ اللَّهِ رَضِيَ اللَّهُ عَنْهُ قَالَكَانُوا يَتَبَايَعُونَ الْجَزُورَ إِلَى حَبَلِ الْحَبَلَةِ فَنَهَى النَّبِيُّ صَلَّى اللَّهُ عَلَيْهِ وَسَلَّمَ عَنْهُ فَسَّرَهُ نَافِعٌ أَنْ تُنْتَجَ النَّاقَةُ مَا فِي بَطْنِهَا عَنْ نَافِعٍ

Concealing the Defects and Cheating

Concealing defects of the sold item and cheating were common widespread practices among the traders in pre-Islamic Arabia. The Prophet (pbAbuh) prohibited these practices and commanded that the seller should disclose the defects of his property. The Prophet is reported to have said: "Surely, whoever deceives (in business) is not one of us."

من غشّ فليس منّا

The Prophet also prohibited giving short measures, which was practice among the people of Madinah in pre-Islamic times.

***Najash* or Fraudulent Overbidding**

Najash refers to an increase in price by a third party who is not actually buying, but wants to encourage others to offer a higher price. It refers to someone's bidding for an item in excess of its price without having any intention of actually buying it but merely in order to induce others to bid still higher prices. Usually, it is pre-arranged for the purpose of deceiving others. *Najash* is prohibited, whereas normal bidding is not.

Price Determination (al-Tas'eer)

There were complaints that the prices of certain items were high and people requested the Prophet (pbAbuh) to fix the prices. He replied: "Allah is the one who fixes price, who withholds, who gives lavishly, and who provides, and I hope that when I meet Him, none of you would have a claim against me for any injustice with regard to blood or property."[12]

الباسط الرزاق وإني لأرجو أن ألقى ربي وليس أحد منكم يطلبني بمظلمة في دم ولا مال
إن الله هو المسعر القابض

The *hadith* indicates that prices are determined by forces that are beyond human control. Prices are determined by the complex market factors over which no individual actor has any control. Those factors include supply, demand, and competitions. These forces propel market toward equilibrium and determine a fair price for commodities, goods, and labour. The *hadith* also indicates that the state should not interfere in the process of price determination. Price determination by the state (*tas'eer*) or any other state interference that disturbs the normal market conditions and equilibrium is harmful. State noninterference in the market is, therefore, a principle.

However, market equilibrium could be disturbed, for instance, by hoarding, meeting the seller on his way to the market (*talaqqial-rukban*), monopolies, underselling, speculation, and collusion among otherwise competitive firms. These practices allow market players to manipulate prices and introduce a degree of artificiality into the market. They act as hindrances to the natural functioning of the market, distort the existing equilibrium, and cause markets to fail. In these situations, state interference is required in order to stop others from interferences and restore the balance in the market. In this way, the true meaning and spirit of the hadith is upheld. Indeed the institution of *hisbah*[13] was established to prevent these hindrances from the natural functioning of the market. The *muhtasib* was responsible to supervise markets and common morals. Among his duties were to check irregularities and to ensure that market players were in the right track and did not indulge in malpractices.[14]

However, during festivals or famine, there could be attempts to hoard essential commodities and create artificial shortages in order to push prices up. In such cases, public interest demands that the state interfere in the market in order to fix the prices of essential items and to make sure that there is enough supply to meet the needs of the people and that no one is hoarding. The state, for example, may introduce price ceiling to control the prices of certain essential items. Similarly, dealers in a certain commodity can be compelled to sell their merchandise, which is needed by the people at a reasonable price. Interference in the market may also be necessitated by monopolies.

In some situations state interference is required in order to stop others from interferences and restore the balance in the market.

Two Sales in One Sale

The Prophet (pbAbuh) has prohibited two transactions in one transaction.[15]

نهى رسول الله صلى الله عليه وسلم عن بيعتين في بيعة

Two sale contracts in one sale refers to a transaction in which a person sells a certain item to a purchaser for an X cash price and a Y deferred price, and the parties do not agree on one specific price, as shown in Figure 1.3. The contract is void as the selling price is not known. However, if the parties agree on a deferred Y price, the transaction does not fall within the definition of two sales in one sale. The principle laid down in this *hadith* is that a sale contract must have one specific price.

If, at the time of bargaining or negotiations, the parties discuss more than one price but finally settle on one price, the sale contract is valid and does not fall within the definition of two sales in one sale. For example, a trader says to a purchaser: If you pay me after one month, the price is RM 50, and if you pay after two months, it will be RM 100. If the trader and the purchaser agree on one of the two prices and a contract is concluded, the transaction will not be prohibited. However, if the parties do not agree on one specific price, the contract falls within the definition of two sales in one sale, and it is prohibited.

FIGURE 1.3 A sale contract must have one price. This sale is void if it has two prices.

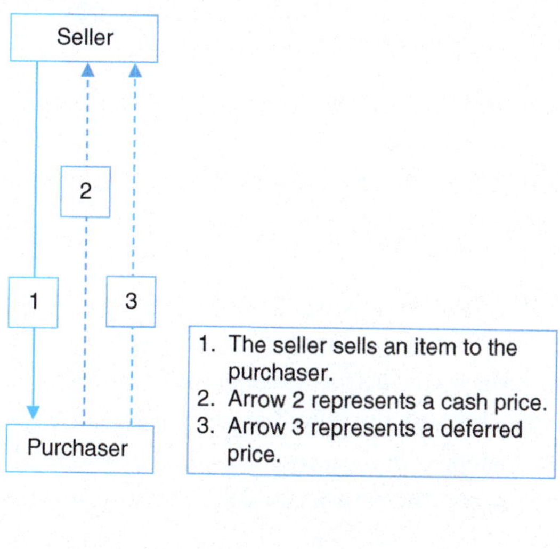

FIGURE 1.4 Sale 1 is concluded on the condition that Sale 2 should take place. As such, Sale 2 is imposed on the party because without it he cannot enter into Sale 1. A sale contract is void when its conclusion depends on another sale.

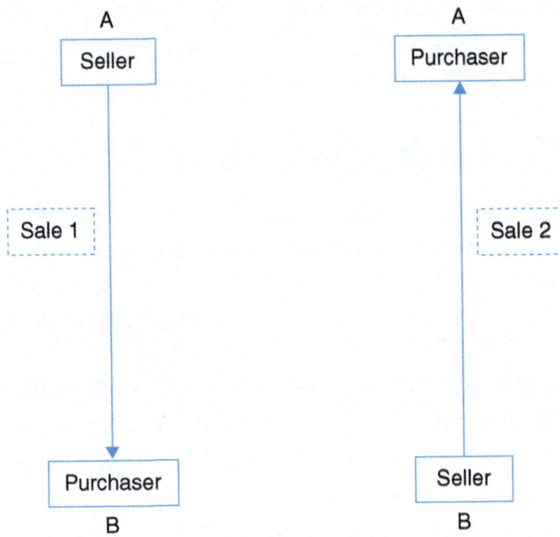

Another meaning of two sales in one sale could be a situation in which the conclusion of one sale contract is made dependent on the conclusion of another sale contract. This is presented in Figure 1.4.

The following is a case study:

Mr. A sells fertilisers to the farmers on a deferred basis at a higher price and stipulates that fertilisers can only be sold to the farmers if they agree to sell him the rice upon harvesting at a price that is fixed in advance but deducted from the price of the fertilisers. The two contracts are not separated from each other. Mr. A is imposing the second contract on the farmers. If the farmer refuses to sell the rice to him, Mr. A will refuse to sell the fertilizers.

Stopping a Seller (Talqi al-Rukban)

Talaqi al-Rukban means meeting a seller who is on his way to a market and buying his merchandise before his arrival at the market. It was a common practice in pre-Islamic time that merchants from the cities would go to the outskirts to meet desert dwellers, who would come to the city to sell their products and to buy commodities that they needed. The Prophet (pbAbuh) prohibited people from buying merchandise from traders before their arrival at the market. He has prohibited this practice by saying, "Do not go to meet the caravans on the way."[16]

The reason for the prohibition could be that the seller who wanted to come to the market may not know the actual market price of the commodity. The purchasers would take advantage of his ignorance because the seller has not yet arrived at the market. It could also be the protection of other traders or purchasers who would be waiting for the arrivals of the sellers and their goods in the market. The reason could also be the protection of the general public.

It is also possible to argue that the reason for the prohibition could be the existence of unnecessary intermediaries between a seller and a potential purchaser. These unnecessary interferences result in increasing prices for a genuine purchaser and a profit to a third party whose intervention is not needed. Third-party intervention neither adds value to the item sold nor makes it more accessible to people.

Contentious Sales

Contentious sales refer to those sales on which there exist differences of opinions among the various *Fiqh* schools and jurists concerning their permissibility or prohibition. In this section, we cover four types of contentious sales and discuss the views and arguments of Muslim jurists for and against them.

*Earnest Money (*Bay' al-'Urbun*)*

'Urbun literally means earnest money or down payment. *Bay' al-'urbun* refers to a sale contract in which a person who wants to purchase a certain property would first pay earnest money to the seller on the condition that, if the sale is executed, the advance payment would go towards the price of the goods, and if the sale is not executed, the down payment is considered a gift from the buyer to the seller.[17] The majority of the *Fiqh* schools rely on a *hadith* that prohibits *bay' al-'urbun*. They also argue that the *bay' al-'urbun* involves ambiguities and uncertainties (*gharar*) and taking another person's money without proper compensation. They consider *bay' al-'urbun* as a prohibited and void (*batil*) contract. According to the Hanafiis, *bay' al-'urbun* is a voidable (*fasid*) contract. According to Imam Ahmad ibn Hanbal, the *hadith* on *bay' al-'urbun* is a weak *hadith*, and he argues for its permissibility based on another *hadith*. The Hanbali jurists have also argued for the permissibility of *'urbun* in a lease contract. However, the *hadith* relied on by the Hanbali jurists is also proven to be weak.[18] Another proof for the validity of *bay' al-urbun* is the following narration by Nafi' ibn 'abd Al-Harith: "He bought for Umar the jailhouse building from Safwanibn 'Umayya for four thousand *Dirhams*, on the condition that if Umar approves it, then the sale is executed, otherwise, Safwan may keep four hundred *Dirhams*."[19]

Because the hadith quoted both by the proponents and opponents of *'urbun* are weak, Wahbah Zuhaili argues for its permissibility on the ground of customs (*'urf*).[20] The Islamic Jurisprudence Council (Majma Al-Fiqh Al-'Islami) in its eighth session in Brunei on the first of Muharram, 1414 A.H., also decided that *bay' al-'urbun* is a permissible contract.

Is 'Urbun *the Sale of Right or a Penalty?*

In *'urbun* the sale contract is not executed and as such the ownership of the property remains with the seller. The payer of the earnest money has the right to purchase the property and can

FIGURE 1.5 A seller receives earnest money and agrees to wait for a specified period within which the payer of the earnest money can purchase the item.

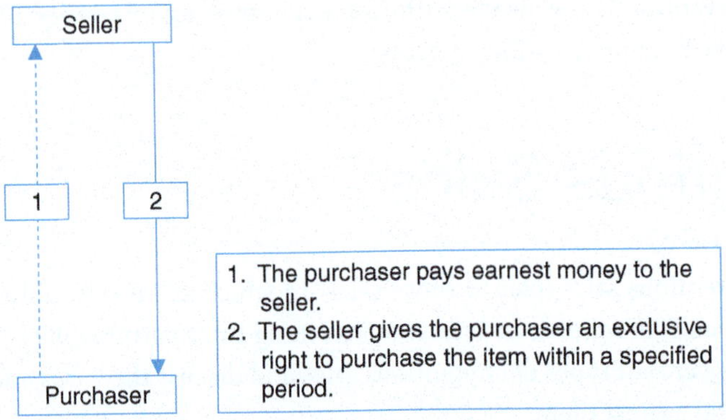

exercise his right within a specified duration. However, the payer of the earnest money is under no obligation to purchase the property. Although the payer of the *'urbun* has the right to purchase the property, the seller is under obligation to sell the property to him within the specified duration. He cannot sell that property to others within that period of time. It is possible to argue that when a person pays earnest money to the seller, he does not purchase the property, but he purchases the right that entitles him to purchase the property within a specified duration. This concept is presented in Figure 1.5. The right lapses if it is not exercised within that duration. Looking from this perspective, *'urbun* entitles a person to an option. If he doesn't exercise the option, he will lose his money. However, if he exercises the option and buys the property, the earnest money would become part of the price. The option is not provided to the seller.

Is *'urbun* a call option in which a purchaser has the right to purchase the item but not the obligation, whereas the seller is obliged to sell the item to the purchaser within a specified period? The difference between *'urbun* and option is that, in the case of *'urbun*, the earnest money is not lost if a property is purchased, whereas in the case of option, the money paid to purchase the option is lost regardless of whether the property is purchased. This distinguishes *'urbun* from option. *'Urbun* acts as an inducement for the buyer to buy the property. It has an encouraging effect because, if the purchaser proceeds with the sale, *'urbun* can become part of the price, whereas in options, the premium paid is forfeited. In some cases the seller needs advance payment in order to cover the initial cost of production. For instance, a caterer may take deposit to cover some of the cost of preparing the foods and to ensure that the order is not cancelled.

Is the seller justified to forfeit the earnest money for cases in which the payer of *'urbun* does not purchase the property? The majority of the *Fiqh* schools oppose *'urbun* on the ground that it entitles the seller to take the money without giving anything in return to the purchaser. However, the seller undertakes not to sell the property to another purchaser within the specified duration. As such, he may lose opportunities to sell the property to others within that period. *'Urbun*, therefore, could be forfeited by the seller due to the loss of opportunities. Because *'urbun* gives a person the right to purchase a property, the ownership of the property still remains with the seller. Consequently, there does not exist a sale contract but only a promise to purchase the property. As such, the forfeiture of 'urbun could be a penalty that a purchaser has to pay for the breach of promise?

> *Because* 'urbun *gives a person the right to purchase a property the ownership of the property still remains with the seller.*

The Sale of Debt (Bay' al-Dayn)

Dayn means "debt" and *bay' al-dayn* means the "sale of debt." *Bay' al-dayn* refers to a contract in which a creditor who has a receivable debt sells it to a third person at a discount. The contract structure is presented in Figure 1.6. The classical Muslim jurists are unanimous that the sale of debt (*bay' al-dayn*) with discount to a third person is not allowed. The majority of the contemporary Muslim scholars and the Islamic Fiqh Academy have also argued that *bay' al-dayn* is a prohibited transaction.[21] However, it is permissible to sell a debt to the debtor himself at a lower price. It could also be sold at its par value to a third person. A creditor may also transfer the debt at its par value to a third person who has sold him goods through the transfer of debt (*hawalah*) contract.

Muslim jurists have argued that *bay' al-dayn* is prohibited on four grounds. These are *riba, gharar,* the absence of possession on the part of the purchaser, and the risks to the purchaser of the debt. First, a debt represents the price of the sold commodity. Thus, if a creditor sells the

FIGURE 1.6 The creditor sells a debt to a third party at a discount. The purchaser of the debt will claim the full amount from the debtor at maturity.

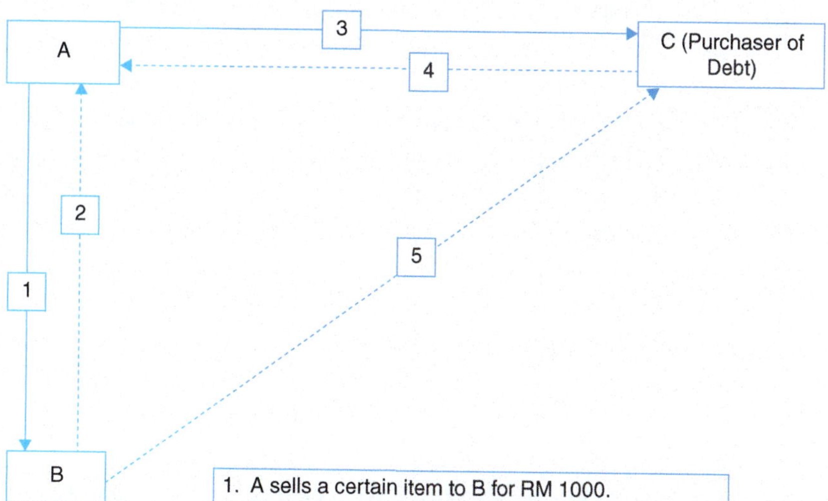

1. A sells a certain item to B for RM 1000.
2. B agrees to pay RM 1000 at a specified date or by instalment.
3. A sells the debt to C for RM 950.
4. C pays RM 950 to the seller.
5. B pays RM 1000 to C on maturity or by instalments.

debt for a discount, it is the sale of money for less money, and as such the transaction violates the conditions of equality and spontaneity set for the exchange for *ribawai* commodities by the *hadith* on *riba al-fadl.* Furthermore, the purchaser of the debt, who buys the debt at a discount, later claims the full amount from the debtor, which may amount to *riba al-nasiyyah.* For instance, a purchaser of a debt pays RM 950 and receives RM 1000 later at the maturity of the debt. Second, due to its abstract and intangible nature, the seller of a debt cannot deliver the debt to the buyer. Because delivery of the debt is not certain, there is an element of *gharar.* The Hanafiis do not include debt (*dayn*) that is a type of claim or a right in their definition of property (*maal*). They argue that debt is not a property (*maal*) but a liability or a claim on a person (*maalhukmi*) that the seller is not able to deliver. Third, possession (*qabad*) of the debt is not possible and as such the purchaser cannot own it. Fourth, the debtor may not be able to settle the debt. It is also possible to argue, as the 2008 economic crisis has shown, that the sale of debt encourages the creation of more debts, subprime debts, and unproductive debts, because the creditors could easily sell their debts in the debt markets. Furthermore, the money will be diverted from investment in the real economy to the debt markets, where there is no real sale and purchase of goods.

There is an argument that a debt that arises from a sale contract can be sold to a third person at a discount. It distinguishes the debt created through a sale contract (*dayn*) from the one created through a loan contract (*qard*). The proponents of this argument contend that a debt represents the sold commodity, and its sale may be taken as the sale of a commodity. They argue that such a debt could lawfully be sold at a discount to others. The creditor may require liquidity and it would create hardships if he is not allowed to sell his debt to others and has to wait till its maturity. The opponents argue that once the commodity is sold, its ownership is passed on to the purchaser, and the seller no longer owns it.

The Shari'ah Advisory Council of the Malaysian Securities Commission, however, contends that securitised debts are different from currencies and cannot be classified under *ribawi* goods. They therefore argue that the transaction is not bound by the conditions for exchanging *ribawi* goods.[22] The Syariah Advisory Council of the Security Commission, after analysing the opinions of the various *Fiqh* schools, argue that the main reason that past Muslim jurists disallowed *bay' al-dayn* "centred on the ability of the seller to deliver the items sold."[23] The Council argues that this may arise in the absence of supervision and control. It was of the opinion that "in the Malaysian context, the debt securities instruments developed according to the principle of *bay' al-dayn* are regulated by Bank Negara Malaysia and the Securities Commission to safeguard the rights of the parties involved in the contract."[24] The Council contended that "the conditions set by the Maliki mazhab and the fears of risks by the Hanafi mazhab can be overcome by regulation and surveillance."[25] The Council concluded that *bay' al-dayn* can be used if there is a regulatory system that protects the buyer and mitigates his risks, and prevent *gharar* and the opportunities for fraud.

Repurchase Sale (Bay' al-'Einah)

Repurchase sale (*bay' al-'einah* or *bai' inah*) is a contract in which a person sells certain goods for a deferred price and repurchases them immediately for a lower cash price from the same person.

Alternatively, he may purchase goods for a cash price and sell them immediately for a higher deferred price to the same person. The following are examples of *bay' al-'einah*:

1. A sells a certain item to B at RM 1100 for a deferred price. A gets a claim of RM 1100, and B gets the sold item. B next sells the same item to A at RM 1000 for a cash payment. Thus, A gets back the item and a claim against B for RM 1100, and B gets RM 1000. The mechanism is presented in Figure 1.7.
2. B sells a certain item to A at RM 1000 for a cash payment. B gets the money and A gets the sold item. A next sells the same item to B at RM 1100 for a deferred price. Thus, B gets back the item and RM 1000, and A has a claim against B for RM 1100. The mechanism is presented in Figure 1.8.
3. B sells to A an article at RM 1100 on credit. A takes the item and sells it to a third party C at a lower price of RM 1000 in cash. C sells it to B at RM 1000. C takes the price from B and gives it to A. B gets his article and A gets RM 1000 in cash. A, however, has to pay RM 1100 to B as the price for the item. The mechanism is presented in Figure 1.9.

FIGURE 1.7 B, who is in need of money, purchases a property from A for a deferred price and resells it to him for a cash price. B would pay the deferred price either in lump sum or by instalment. B got the cash and the item is reverted to A.

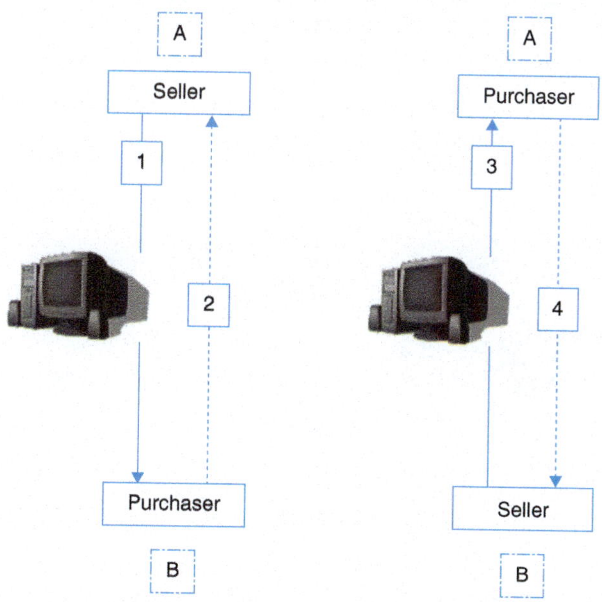

1. A sells an item to B for a deferred price of RM 1100.
2. B agrees to pay the price of RM 1100 either by instalment or lump sum at a future specified time.
3. B next sells the same item to A for cash payment.
4. A pays RM 1000 in cash.

FIGURE 1.8 B, who is in need of money, sells his property to A for a cash price and repurchases it for a deferred price. B would pay the deferred price either in lump sum or by instalment. B got the cash, and the property is also reverted to him.

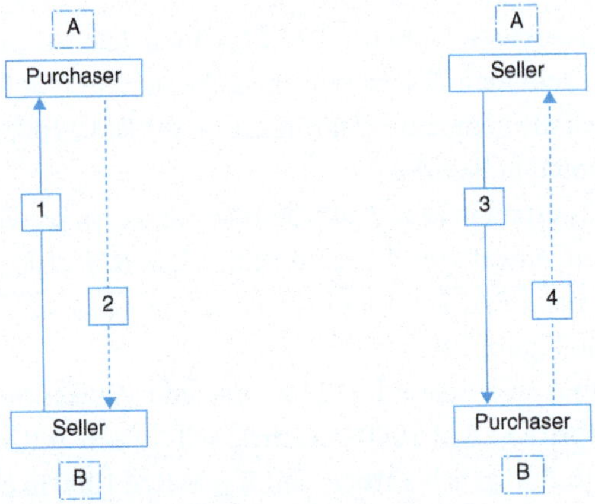

1. B sells an item to A for a cash price of RM 1000.
2. A pays the price of RM 1000 in cash.
3. A next sells the same item to B for a deferred price of RM 1100.
4. B pays RM 1100 either by instalment or lump sum at a future specified date.

FIGURE 1.9 B, who is in need of money, purchases a property from A for a deferred price and sells it to C for cash. C sells the same item to A for cash. B got the cash and the item is reverted to A.

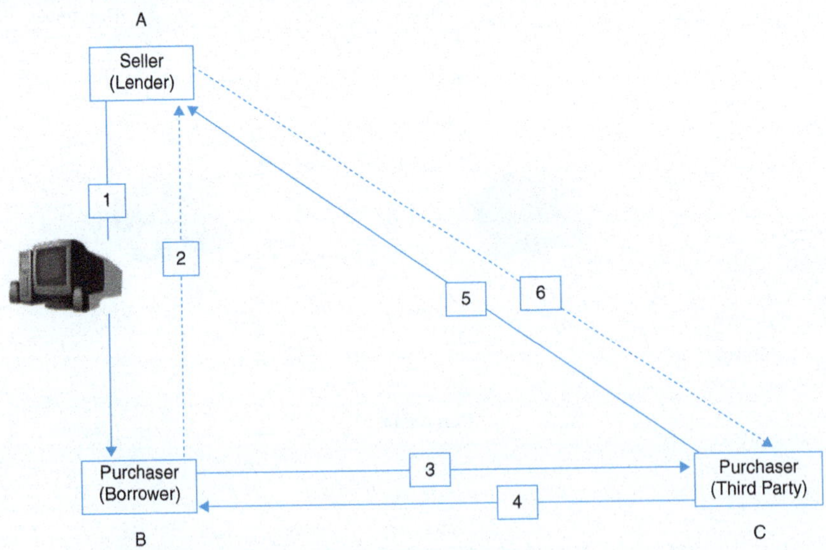

1. A sells an item to B.
2. B agrees to pay the price of RM 1100 by instalment.
3. A next sells the item to C (the third party).
4. C pays the price of RM 1000 in cash.
5. C next sell the item to A in cash.

A sale contract is normally used to meet the mutual needs of the parties for the sold item and the price. However, the parties enter into a repurchase agreement (*ba'y al-'einah*) whereby one of them sells a certain asset for deferred payment and repurchases the same asset for a lower cash price. The purpose for which the two sales are concluded is not to purchase the item, because it reverts to the initial owner, but to provide cash to one of the parties who would later have to pay a higher deferred price. However, when a contract of such a nature is concluded, all its pillars and conditions concerning the offer and acceptance, the contracting parties, and the subject matter are fulfilled. The unlawful purpose itself or the second contract is never referred to in the agreement.

The question that could be raised here is whether the validity of a contract depends on the fulfillment of its pillars and conditions or we have to look behind the agreement to the hidden intention or motive of the contracting parties. Does the existence of an unlawful motive behind a permissible contract make a contract invalid? Can bad or good intention or motive determine the validity of a contract? Should we also take into account the hidden intention and purpose of the contracting parties while determining the validity of a contract? This gave rise to the debate on the question of motive and intention of the contracting parties. Muslim jurists are divided into two groups on the issue of unlawful hidden intention or purpose. One group looks at the purpose of the parties as expressed in the agreement, whereas the other group looks at the hidden purpose of the parties that is not expressed but could be understood from the context. The Shafi'is and the Hanafis look at the agreement itself and the purpose of the parties as expressed in the agreement. They don't look beyond the agreement at the hidden intention or motive of the contracting parties. They argue that the *Shari'ah* requires that the parties should enter into a certain permissible contract by mutual consent and fulfil all its pillars and conditions. According to them, the bad purpose or hidden intention of the contracting parties does not affect its validity unless it is expressly or implicitly mentioned in the agreement and becomes one of its terms and conditions. They further contend that the hidden intention or purpose/motive of the parties is personal to the parties and may change from one person to another and from a contract to a contract. The parties may intend to use *bay' al-einah* to avoid *riba* or they may intend to use it to circumvent the injunctions against *riba*. It would be unfair to make a general rule that would apply to all cases, because the hidden intention or motive cannot be known and is left to Allah (swt). The majority of the Hanafii and Shafi'i jurists are of the opinion that *bay' al-einah* is a contractually correct (*sahih*) agreement if it fulfils the pillars and the necessary conditions of a sale contract. Thus, a court may decide that it is valid on technical grounds. The hidden intentions of the parties, which is not expressed or referred to in the contract, is irrelevant for a judge when deciding on the validity of a contract. However, *bay' al-einah* is forbidden (*haram*) according to the Hanafii jurists and abominable (*makruh*) according to the Shafi'i jurists if the parties intend to use it to circumvent the prohibition of *riba*. Muhammad Al-Shaybani from the Hanafii school was of the opinion that *bay' al-einah* is a valid but reprehensible (*makruh*) contract. He said, "The dislike for this sale in my heart is as heavy as mountains; it was invented by those who devour *riba*."[26]

The Maliki and Hanbalii jurists, on the other hand, have prohibited *bay' al-'einah* emphatically. They take into account not only the contractual requirements but also the hidden intention or the motive of the parties while deciding on the validity of *bay' al-'einah*. This group of jurists takes into account the purpose or intention/motive of the parties even if it is not mentioned in the agreement provided one of the parties knows that the other party has an unlawful purpose or motive or has the means to know through indications and circumstances surrounding the contract. They argue that the hidden intention of the parties could be judged from their subsequent actions. According to them, if the motive of the parties is unlawful, the contract is also void, and vice versa. They argue that the profit in a repurchase sale (*bay'al-'einah*) is similar to lending charges or interest added to a loan. They therefore use the juristic method of blocking the means (*sadd al-dharai'*), a method that they have introduced to Islamic jurisprudence (*usul al-fiqh*) to prohibit *bay' al-'einah* because it is used as a means that leads to prohibited ends.[27] According to the doctrine of *sadd al-dharai'*, a permissible means could be prohibited if it is expected to lead to an unlawful end.[28] According to this principle, the intention of the parties or the actual realisation of the evil result are irrelevant in determining the status of the means. If a certain means could lead to a prohibited (*haram*) end, the means will also be prohibited (*haram*).[29] However, if the object of sale has changed or depreciated, then the repurchase by the original seller for a new price is valid and it is not considered as *bay' al-einah.*[30]

The main problem with *bay' al-enah* is that it is a fictitious or fake sale contract. Fake sale contracts are not tied to the real economy, and the price of the sold item does not reflect its market value. As such, these contracts do not contribute to economic development but only create more debts. They also increase the gap between the real economy and the inflated financial system. The seller and the purchaser do not enter into the sale contract for the sake of the sold item, but, rather, they want to use the sale contract as a means to provide cash to one of the parties. It is a legal trick (*hilah*) to provide cash and receive an extra amount that is the real intention of the contracting parties. *Hila* refers to a legal device or fiction employed to avoid a direct violation of Islamic law. These legal fictions were mainly used to enable an individual to indirectly achieve a certain result that he could not directly achieve because of *Shari'ah* prohibition.

*Tripartite Sale (*Bay' al-Tawarruq*)*

Bay' al-tawarruq, also known as a commodity *murabaha,* is a contract in which a person purchases certain goods/commodities at a deferred higher price in order to sell it in the market to a third party for a lower cash price. This definition refers to a classical form of the *tawarruq* contract, which is considered permissible provided it meets the other requirement and conditions of the sale contract. In this type of classical *tawarruq,* as presented in Figure 1.10, there is no prior arrangement between the parties. B purchases the item from A and then sells it in the market to a third party. In this form of simple *tawarruq,* the parties, by going to the market, enter into real transactions. According to Ibn Taymiyya and Ibn Qayim Al-Jauziyah, the contract is classified as abominable (*makruh*). Ibn Taymiyya saw *tawarruq* as "the little sister of *riba.*"[31] *Tawarruq* is only allowed if a person under dire necessity urgently needs cash that he cannot obtain through other permissible contracts.

In an organised *tawarruq,* a customer approaches an Islamic bank for an amount of money. The bank purchases a commodity for cash and sells it to a customer at a deferred higher price.

FIGURE 1.10 B asks A to lend him RM 1000. A does not want to lend him money. Instead, A would sell to B an item for RM 1100 for a deferred price. The item, however, can be sold in the market for RM 1000. B buys the item from A for RM 1100 and sells that in the market for RM 1000. Thus, B gets the cash but he has to pay A RM 1100 as the deferred price for the item. The price could be paid in a lump sum or by instalments.

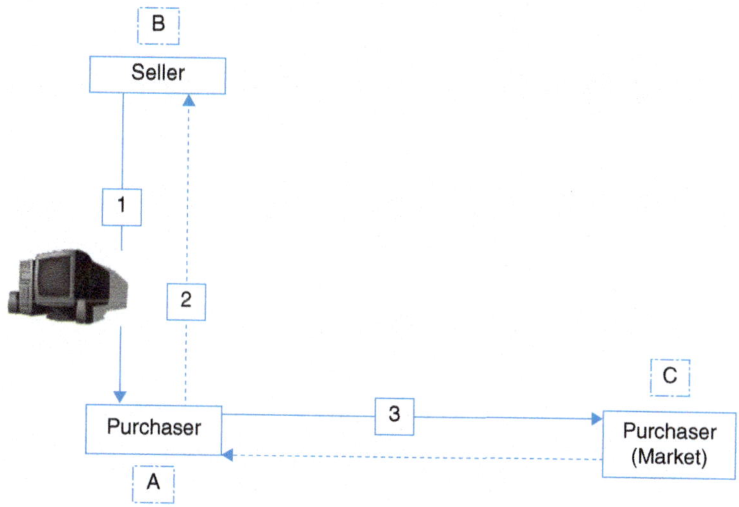

1. B sells an item to A for RM 1100.
2. A agrees to pay the price by instalments.
3. A sells the item for a cash price of RM 1000 in the market to a third person C.
4. C pays A RM 1000 in cash.

The customer agrees to pay the amount in an agreed number of instalments. The customer subsequently appoints the bank as an agent to sell the same commodity in the market for a cash price. The bank sells the commodity on behalf of the customer and transfers the price to him. The contract structure is presented in Figure 1.11.

However, the way *twarruq* was implemented by the Islamic bank raised serious questions about its validity. In its organised form the transaction may not be real and may only exist in papers. A client approaches a bank for an amount of money and agrees to repay it with an agreed mark-up in a number of instalments. The bank purchases a commodity in cash and sells it to the customer for a higher deferred price. The customer does not know whether the bank owns the commodity and he is not interested in the commodity itself. The bank next would sell the commodity on behalf of the customer and deposit the proceeds in the customer's account. The sequence of transactions is not observed and is repeated for many customers in a single day. The customer merely signs the documents.

The International Council of Fiqh Academy of the Organization of Islamic Cooperation (OIC) in its 19th session, which was held in Sharjah, United Arab Emirate, from 1–5 of

FIGURE 1.11 The customer, who needs cash, agrees to purchase a certain commodity from the bank. The bank purchases the commodity in the commodity market and sells it to the customer for a deferred price. The customer, who now owns the commodity, appoints the bank to act as an agent and sells the commodity in the market. The bank sells the commodity for a cash price and returns the money to the customer. The customer has obtained the needed cash but he has to pay the bank the deferred price of the commodity.

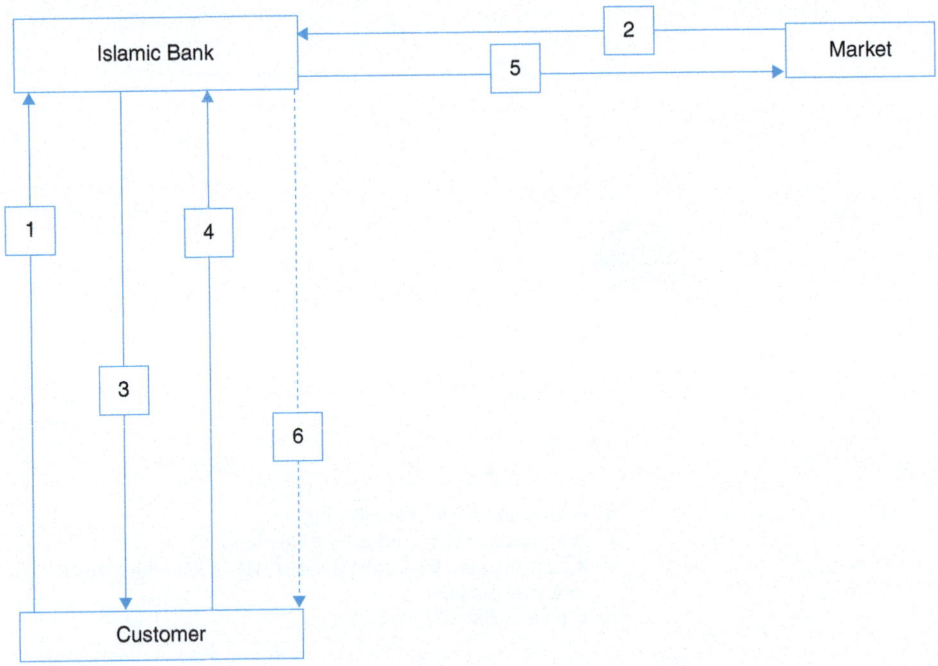

1. The customer needs RM 10,000 and approaches an Islamic bank.
2. The bank purchases a certain commodity from the market for cash RM 10,000.
3. The bank sells the commodity to the customers for a deferred price of RM 1100 payable in a year.
4. The customer appoints the bank as an agent to sell the commodity on his behalf in the market.
5. The bank sells the commodity for RM 10,000 in cash in the market.
6. The bank transfers RM 10,000 to the customers.

Jamadil Ula 1430 A.H., corresponding to April 26–30, 2009, has decided that organised *tawarruq* is not permissible because it involves simultaneous transactions between the bank and the customer. The Council held that the transaction involves deception in order to get additional quick cash and contain elements of *riba* (usury).[32]

In its organised form the tawarruq transaction may not be real and may only exist in papers.

It is possible to argue that *tawarruq* could be used only for limited purposes and in case of necessities when money could not be obtained through loan (*qard hasan*) and other permissible contracts. These necessities may include marriage, medical treatment, urgent travel for legitimate needs, and other similar necessities. *Tawarruq* could be used in such cases to provide money to the persons in need and in order to avoid interest-bearing loans.

The banks should ensure that the commodities in question can be locally acquired where the customer can actually take possession, see, and inspect them. The customer should also dispose of the commodity by selling it himself or through his agent. The banks should not dispose of the commodity on behalf of the customers so that the contracts remain real.

Chapter Questions

True/False

1. ( ) If a purchaser fails to pay the price, the seller can cancel the sale contract.
2. ( ) It is possible for a seller and a buyer to mutually agree that the seller will sell his house for one year after which the buyer should again sell the house to him.
3. ( ) A seller may sell his house on the condition that the purchaser should rent out the same house to him.
4. ( ) If a purchaser fails to pay the price, the seller can cancel the sale contract and fix another price.
5. ( ) In *bay' al-'urbun,* the seller is exposed to price risk because the property may not be sold for the same price.
6. ( ) In *bay' al-'urbun,* the right to purchase the property is sold to the purchaser and not the property itself.
7. ( ) In sale of debt (*bay al-dayn*), there is an element of uncertainty (*gharar*) because the seller is not delivering the debt.
8. ( ) In a sale of debt, the purchaser of the debt agrees to exchange some money now for more money later.
9. ( ) In sale of debt (*bay al-dayn*), there is an element of uncertainty (*gharar*) because the debtor may not be able to pay the debt.
10. ( ) If a debt is sold to a third person, this would burden the debtor because he has to pay more to the third person.
11. ( ) In sale of debt (*bay' al-dayn*), the payment of the debt to the purchaser of the debt is guaranteed.
12. ( ) The difference between *bay' al-einah* and *tawarruq* is that in *tawarruq* the sold item is repurchased by the same seller.
13. ( ) A person can sell certain goods that he does not own provided he is certain to acquire those goods and deliver them to the purchaser.

14. ( ) A sale contract cannot have two prices—one for cash payment and another for deferred payment.
15. ( ) The reason for the prohibition of *talaqi al-rukban* could be to prevent all unnecessary interferences between a seller and a potential purchaser.

Short Answer

1. In a contract of sale, price is distinguished from the thing sold. What are the main consequences that may follow from this distinction?
2. Earnest money (*bay' al-urboon*) is one of the contentious contracts on which *Fiqh* schools have divergent opinions. Define and briefly discuss the various arguments for and against *bay' al-urboon.*
3. Jurists argue against the sale of debt (*bay' al-dayn*) to a third party with a discount. Discuss the main reasons for their arguments.
4. The majority of Muslim jurists hold the view that *bay' al-'einah* is a circumvention of the rule that prohibits usury (*riba*). Explain why they consider it so? Support your answer with relevant examples.
5. *Talaqi al-rukban* (stopping the rider) was a practice that was prohibited by the Prophet (pbAbuh). Analyse the reason behind the prohibition and provide contemporary examples.
6. Can we argue against speculation on the ground that it interferes with the prices?
7. A monopolist determines and dictates the prices of goods he is selling. In your opinion, what is the best approach to deal with monopolies?
8. The forces of supply and demand and the interaction of maximising agents bring markets towards equilibrium. In your opinion, what are the forces that disturb this equilibrium?

Notes

1. The *Qur'an*, 4:29.
2. The *Qur'an*, 2:275.
3. Musnad Ahmad, *Hadith Rafe' bin Khadiz*, vol. 37, no. 17728: 217.
4. Sunan Ibn Majah, *Bab al-Bay' al- Khiyar*, vol. 7, no. 2269: 10.
5. Wahbah Zuhaili, *al-Fiqh al-Islami Wa Adillatahu* 4: 93. See also Muhammad Yusuf Saleem, *An Introduction to the Theoretical Foundations of Islamic Transactions* (Selangor: Ilmiah Publishers, 2010), 84–86.
6. See also *The Mejelle*, Articles 985–987, which states that both males and females attain the age of majority at 15.
7. Zuhaili, *al-Fiqh al-Islami Wa Adillatahu*, 389.
8. Ibid.
9. See M. Muhsin Khan (trans.), *Sahih Bukhari* vol. 3, book 50, no. 879.
10. Zuhaili, *al-Fiqh al-Islami Wa Adillatuhu*, 203.

11. M. Muhsin Khan (trans.), *Sahih-al-bukhari*; vol. 3, book 35, no 2256 (Riyadh: Darussalam, 1997).
12. Sunan al-Tirmidhi, *Babu Ma Jaya fi al-Tassayir*, vol. 5, no. 1362: 278. See also Yusuf al-Qaradawi, *The Lawful and the Prohibited in Islam*, trans. Kamal El-Helbawy (Kuala Lumpur: Islamic Book Trust, 1995), 255.
13. The history of the institution of *hisbah* goes back to the time of the Prophet (pbAbuh). It remained in existence throughout the greater part of the Muslim world until the beginning of the twentieth century. The officer in charge of the *hisbah* was called *muhtasib*. For a discussion see Abdul Azim Islahi, *Economic Concepts of Ibn Taimiyah* (Leicester: The Islamic Foundation, 1988), 186–191.
14. See Muhammad Yusuf Saleem, "Methods and Methodologies in Fiqh and Islamic Economics," *Review of Islamic Economics* 14, no. 1 (2010): 103–123.
15. Sunan al-Tirmizi, 2/514.
16. Khan, *Sahih Bukhari*, vol.3, book 34, no. 367.
17. See as-Sayyid Sabiq, *Fiqh as-Sunnah* (Cairo: Dar al-Hadith, 2004), 917–918.
18. For a discussion, see Wahbah al-Zuhaili, *Financial Transactions in Islamic Jurisprudence*, vol.1, trans. Mahmoud A. El-Gamal (Beirut: Dar al-Fikr al-Mouaser, 2003), 99–100.
19. *Ibn Qudamah* (vol.4, 232); Al-Sanhuris, *Masadir Al-Haqq* (vol.2, 96ff), Professor Mustafa Al-Zarqa, *Al-Madkhal Al-Fiqh* (section 234).
20. al-Zuhaili, *Financial Transactions in Islamic Jurisprudence*, 100.
21. See Muhammad Taqi Usmani, *An Introduction to Islamic Finance* (Karachi: Maktaba Ma'ariful Qur'an, 2004), 216–218.
22. See Resolutions of the Securities Commission Syariah Advisory Council (Kuala Lumpur: Securities Commission, 2002), 19.
23. Ibid.
24. Ibid.
25. Ibid.
26. See al-Zuhaili, *Financial Transactions in Islamic Jurisprudence*, 115. See also Zuhaili, *al-Fiqh al-Islami Wa Adillatuhu*, 186.
27. Ibid, 115–116.
28. Mohammad Hashim Kamali, *Principles of Islamic Jurisprudence*, 2nd ed. (Kuala Lumpur: Ilmiah Publishers, 2004), 310–311.
29. Ibid, 311.
30. See Abu al-Walid Muhammad ibn Ahmad ibn Rushd, *Bidayat al-Mujtahid wa Nihayat al-Muqtasid*, vol.2 (Beirut: Dar al-Kutub al-'Ilmiyyah, 2003), 227.
31. Dar Al Salam, *Fatawa Al Imam Ibn Taimiyya fi Al Muamalatwa Al Ahkam Al Mal* (Cairo, 2005), 337. Available at www.dar-alsalam.com.
32. For a discussion, see Mohammed Obaidullah, *Islamic Financial Services* (Jeddah: Islamic Economics Research Centre, 2003), 109–112.

CHAPTER 2

Types and Classifications of Sales

Learning outcomes

At the end of this chapter, you should be able to:

1. Explain the two main classifications of a sale contract.
2. Understand the various types of trust sales in which the cost price of the sold item is disclosed to the purchaser.
3. Understand the deferred sale contract in which the price is postponed or paid by installments.
4. Understand how an Islamic bank would enter into a sale contract with a customer and how this sale is different from the interest-bearing loan contract.
5. Explain future commodity sale (*salam*), manufacturing sale (*istisna'*), and currency exchange (*sarf*) sale.
6. Distinguish between *salam* and *istisna'* contracts and between *salam* and future and forward contracts.
7. Understand how an Islamic bank may enter into *salam* and *istisna'* contracts with their clients.

Introduction

Sale contracts could be classified in two different ways, as shown in Figure 2.1. The first classification is based on how the price of the sold property is determined. If a property is sold for a price mutually agreed by the parties without any reference to its cost price, the contract is considered a bargain (*musawamah*) sale. A bargain (*musawamah*) sale is the most commonly used sale in which the price of the sold item is determined by the seller and the purchaser based on bargaining and mutual agreement. The seller is not obliged to disclose his cost price. If a property is sold with reference to its cost, price the contract is considered trust (*amanah*) sale.

The second classification is based on the time the price is paid and the subject matter is delivered. Generally speaking, in all sale contracts the subject matter should be delivered immediately, whereas the price could be paid on the spot, by instalments, or deferred to a future date. However, in some sale contracts such as in deferred delivery sale (*salam*) the price should be paid on the spot and should not be deferred, whereas the subject matter is delivered at a future date. In a sale of currency for another (*sarf*), both currencies should be exchanged on the

FIGURE 2.1 Sale contracts are mainly classified in two ways, based on the mode of payment and the disclosure of the cost price. In a *Bay' Bi-thaman Aajil* (BBA), the price is postponed or paid by instalment, in a *salam* sale the price is paid on the spot, whereas in a *sarf*, both prices must be paid on the spot. A price could also be determined based on bargain between the parties or based on the original cost.

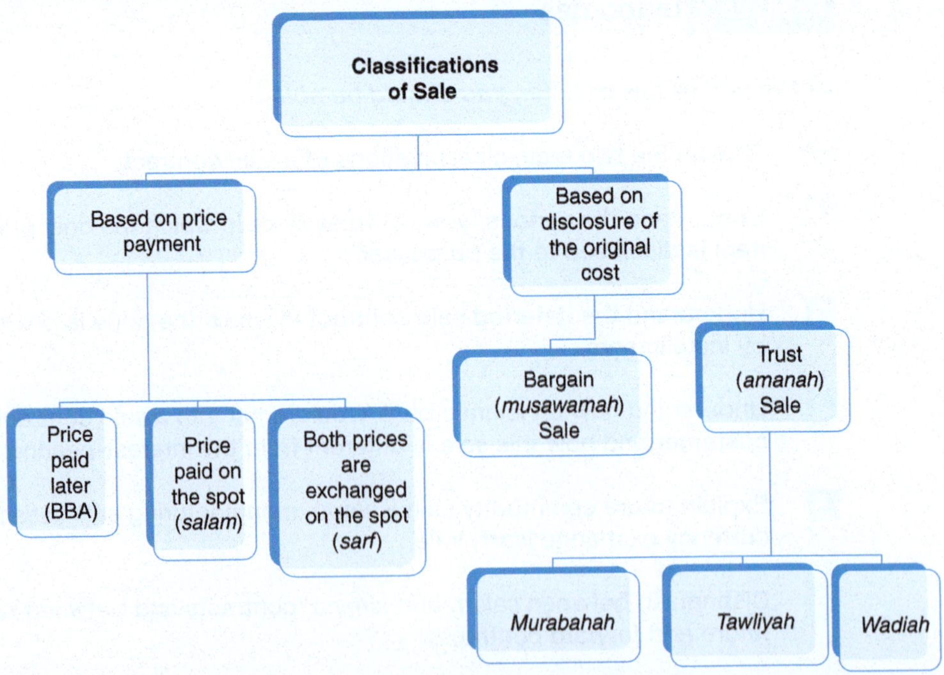

spot. In a manufacturing sale (*istisna*), both the payment of the price and the delivery of the sold item can be postponed to a future date.

Trust Sales (*Buyu' al-amanah*)

As mentioned earlier, trust sales (*buyu' al-amanah*) are a type of sales in which the seller is under obligation to disclose to the purchaser the cost price. The main purpose for which trust sales are used is the protection of purchasers and consumers who lack expertise and knowledge about certain goods and their prices. Due to his lack of knowledge, the purchaser needs and agrees to buy goods based on trust sale from a seller who is supposed to have sufficient knowledge about the quality and price of the goods. In return, the purchaser agrees to pay a certain agreed upon additional amount over and above the cost price to the seller as a profit. Since the purchaser relies on the words of the seller, the seller has to be just and truthful to his words and abstain from fraud or misinformation. If the seller is guilty of any deception, the purchaser is entitled to cancel the contract provided the property is not destroyed or damaged before he returns it. Thus, a trust sale is intended to protect the interests of commercially unsophisticated purchasers. Trust sales are further subdivided into cost-plus-profit sale (*murabahah*), sale with no profit (*tawliyah*), and sale with loss (*wadi'ah*). In all these sales, the selling price must be based on the cost price.

Cost-plus-Profit Sale (Murabahah)

Murabahah is derived from the root word *ribh,* which literally means profit. It refers to a sale contract in which goods are sold for their cost price plus a specified mark-up or profit agreed upon by the parties. *Murabahah* is the resale of goods at some profit added on the original cost. The seller transfers the ownership of his property, which he had acquired at a certain price to the buyer with an agreed increment to the price. The mark-up may be a lump sum or a certain percentage of the purchase price. For example, goods can be sold at a relative profit as 11 for 10, or 10 percent profit. The profit is made to cover the cost of maintaining, storage, and transportation. The profit made could also be used to pay employees who looked after the goods. Whether to include these costs in the original price or to deduct them from the profit depend on the agreement between the parties. The profit is made for the expertise and efforts that the seller provides. After basing the sale's price on the original cost of the goods to the seller, the purchaser is provided with a degree of protection against unjust exploitation. When a person purchases a thing on credit, before he sells it by *murabahah* he should inform the purchaser of the fact, because when a property is bought on credit, its price is necessarily higher than the cash price.

The most important conditions of the *murabahah* sale are:

- The seller has to disclose the original cost of the goods including all the expenses.
- The purchaser should know the amount of the profit whether it is a fixed amount or a percentage of the cost price.

- The first sale contract must be valid. For instance, if the first seller was bankrupt or sold a property that was pledged, the *murabahah* contract will be cancelled.
- The seller is under obligation to inform the purchaser of any defect in the goods. If the purchaser discovers that the goods are defective, he either can ask for compensation or a cancellation of the sale.

*Sale With No Profit (*Tawliyah*)*

The word *tawliyah* implies protection and guardianship because the seller is delegating ownership of the goods to the purchaser without any profit. The seller sells the goods to the purchaser for the price for which he had originally purchased them, without any profit or loss.

*Sale With Loss (*Wadi'ah*)*

The word *wadi'ah* literally means loss. In *wadi'ah,* the seller discloses the original cost of the goods but sells them with a loss. The loss may be a lump sum or a certain percentage of the purchase price, for example, when goods are sold for 10 percent loss based on their cost price.

Deferred Payment Sale (*Bay' Bi-thaman Aajil*)

Bay' Bi-thaman Aajil (BBA) is a sale contract in which the sold property is delivered to the purchaser upon signing the sale agreement, whereas the price is postponed to a future date or paid by instalments. The date for the future payment, the duration of instalment, and the amount payable in each instalment should be clear and known to the parties. A deferred sale contract could either be a bargain (*musawamah*) sale, in which the cost price is not disclosed, or it should be a trust (*amanah*) sale, in which the cost price is disclosed to the purchaser. Can a seller increase the price of goods if the purchaser asks for deferred payment or wants to pay by instalments? There are two views on this issue. The proponents say that a sale transaction, in which the deferred price is higher than the cash price, is similar to a loan contract in which a borrower has to pay an additional amount to the lender due to the deferred time. They argue that the price increase is due to the time delay that resembles interest because interest is also an additional amount paid for time. They argue, therefore, that this is recognition of the time value of money and amounts to usury (*riba*). The proponents argue that the basic principle in transactions is permissibility (*ibahah*). Accordingly, they argue that a deferred price could be higher than the spot price because the *Qur'an* and the *Sunnah* have not prohibited it. They further argue that the seller and purchaser are free to agree on a price as long as it does not amount to exploitation or clear injustice.[1] TaqiUsmani contends that an increase of price in a deferred sale contract is not usury because, in usury, money is exchanged for more money, whereas in a deferred sale, a commodity is sold for a higher price. He argues that "Any excess amount charged against late payment is *riba* only where the subject matter is money on both sides."[2] He further argues that the fixed price in a sale contract relates to the sold property and not to the time. If a purchaser fails to pay the instalments or defaults, the seller cannot increase the price.[3]

Islamic Banks and a Sale Contract

A customer identifies a property and requests the seller to send a quotation. He then approaches an Islamic bank and requests the bank to purchase the property for a subsequent sale to him. The bank studies the request and negotiates the selling price, mode of payment, duration of instalments, and other conditions and securities. The bank undertakes to purchase the property as requested by the customer and resells it to him.

A sale contract between an Islamic bank and a purchaser (customer) is usually preceded by a promise made by the customer to purchase the property. The bank will not purchase a property unless the customer promises to buy it. A promise is needed as the customer later may refuse to purchase the property. It is also needed because the bank does not own the property and cannot enter into a valid sale contract with the customer. The customer promises that, if the bank purchases the property, he will buy it from the bank on the basis of *murabahah.*

The selling price includes the cost price plus a margin of profit agreed upon during the promise stage. The margin of profit is decided by the duration of financing period. The selling price is known from the time the contract is signed and cannot be altered. The payment will be settled by the customer at a future agreed upon date, either in lump sum or instalments.

The bank should act as a trader and not as a financier. It is necessary that the bank should buy and own the property before it is sold to the purchaser. The risk of the transaction is born by the bank until the ownership of the property is transferred to the customer and the property is delivered to him. Profit is justified because it is derived from buying and selling of properties as opposed to interests charged on lending money.

The following conditions should also be observed when Islamic banks conclude sale contracts with their customers:

- The bank should acquire ownership and possession of the goods prior to its sale to the purchaser.
- The bank must carry the risk of loss before delivery.
- The bank must bear the consequences of rejection of the goods by the buyer if he exercises his option to cancel the contract because of concealed defects.
- Promise from any of the two parties of the contract is morally binding on both the parties. However, if the bank, while relying on the promise, takes the necessary steps to acquire the property, then the promise becomes legally binding.[4]

The bank should act as a trader and not as a financier. It is necessary that the bank should buy and own the property before it is sold to the purchaser.

Differences between a *murabahah*/BBA sale and an interest-based loan include:

- *Murabahah* is based on a sale contract, whereas conventional financing is based on an interest-based loan in which a bank advances a loan and charges interest. The relationship between an Islamic bank and the customer is one of seller and purchaser, whereas in conventional banking, it is one of creditor and borrower.

FIGURE 2.2 In conventional banking, a customer has to sign two contracts: one with the developer for the purchase of a house and the other with the bank for obtaining the loan. However, in Islamic banking, the customer has to sign only one contract with the bank for the purchase of the house.

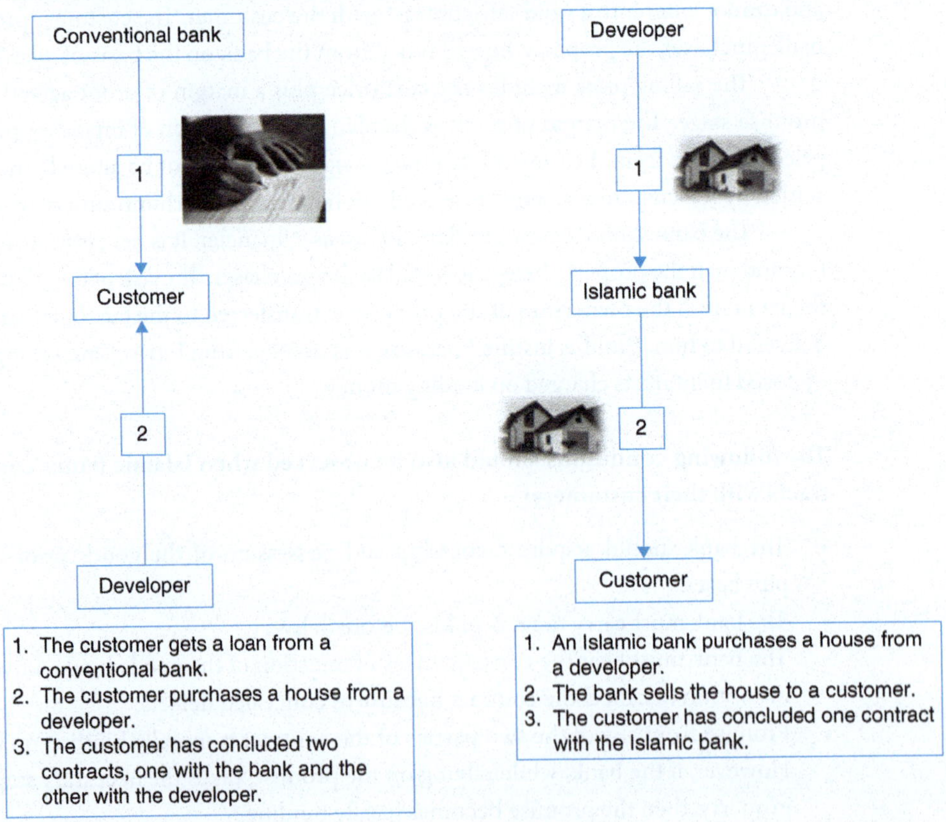

- In *murabahah*, the price of the sold asset is fixed, whereas the amount paid by the borrower to the conventional bank may depend on the rate of interest, which fluctuates.
- In conventional banking, in case of default of payment, the borrower will be charged interest on interest as the arrears are be capitalised. However, in Islamic banking, the bank may sue the purchaser for default but cannot increase the price.
- The purchaser from an Islamic bank should be entitled to the various options that enable him to cancel the contract. This issue does not arise in conventional banking because the contract between the parties is a loan contract.
- In the case of a *murabahah* or BBA contract, the customer has only one contract with the bank, as shown in Figure 2.2. He does not have direct contractual relationship with a seller from whom the bank has purchased the property. If a *murabahah* contract is declared void by the courts on grounds of defect, fraud, or misrepresentation (where, for example, the developer has built lower quality houses), the bank would have to suffer the consequences. However, in conventional banking, a customer has two contracts: the contract of loan between the bank and the customer and the contract of sale between the customer and the seller. If the contract of sale is declared void for some reason, the customer still has to settle his debt to the bank. In other words, a conventional bank does not take any risk.

Some of the reasons behind *murabahah's* popularity include the following:

- It is a sale contract in which the ownership with all its obligations—for instance, insurance, maintenance, and taxes—is transferred to the purchaser.
- It generates a certain specified fixed amount of debt, unlike a partner's right to share in future profit, which is not known.
- As a debt obligation, it can be secured through mortgages or pledge (*rahn*).
- Compared to partnership, it reduces the need to monitor the customer's business or trust his honesty.

Future Commodity Sale (*Bay' al-Salam*)

Salam, or *salaf*, means prepayment. *Salam* is a sale transaction in which the price of a specified amount of a commodity deliverable at an agreed upon future time is paid immediately upon signing the contract. For example, a purchaser pays RM 10,000 in cash upon signing the *salam* contract, and the seller agrees to supply 5000 kg of grade A rice at a specified future time and place, as shown in Figure 2.3. Because payment is made on the spot, the contract price could be lower than the market price. The prohibition of the Prophet (pbAbuh) that a person should not sell what he does not have does not apply to *salam* contract. The prohibition applies only to those goods that are readily available in the market. If goods are readily available in the market, the seller must own them and be capable of delivering them. The transaction is prohibited if a seller does not own such goods. Salam is permitted based on need, especially in the agriculture sector, where a farmer may need advance payment of the price to finance his activities. The farmer is capable of fulfiling a *salam* undertaking at a certain specified time in future.

FIGURE 2.3 A specified amount of rice of a known quality is sold for future delivery. The price is paid on the spot.

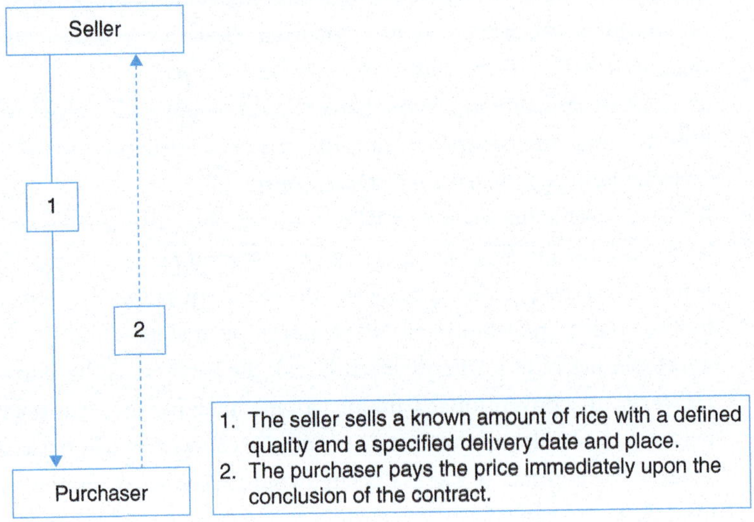

In the pre-Islamic period, *salam* was practised by selling a certain crop in a specific field without specifying the measure, weight, and date of its delivery. The contract in this form contained elements of *gharar* and was prohibited. Improvements to the contract were made in order to remove the elements of *gharar*. Ibn 'Abbas (mAbpwt) narrated: "The Prophet (pbAbuh) came to Medina and the people used to pay in advance the price of dates to be delivered within two or three years. He said (to them), 'Whoever pays in advance the price of a thing (fruits or grains) to be delivered later should pay it for a specified measure at specified weight for a specified period'."[5]

رَضِيَ اللَّهُ عَنْهُمَا قَالَقَدِمَ النَّبِيُّ صَلَّى اللَّهُ عَلَيْهِ وَسَلَّمَ الْمَدِينَةَ وَهُمْ يُسْلِفُونَ بِالتَّمْرِ السَّنَتَيْنِ وَالثَّلَاثَ فَقَالَ مَنْ أَسْلَفَ
فِي شَيْءٍ فَفِي كَيْلٍ مَعْلُومٍ وَوَزْنٍ مَعْلُومٍ إِلَى أَجَلٍ مَعْلُومٍ عنْ ابْنِ عَبَّاسٍ

Muhammad bin Al-Majalid (mAbpwh) narrated:

> Abdullah bin Shaddad and Abu Burda sent me to 'Abdullah bin Abi Aufa and told me to ask 'Abdullah whether the people in the life-time of the Prophet used to pay in advance for wheat (to be delivered later). Abdullah replied, "We used to pay in advance to the peasants of Sham for wheat, barley and olive oil of a known specified measure to be delivered in a specified period." I asked (him), "Was the price paid (in advance) to those who had the things to be delivered later?" Abdullah bin Aufa replied, "We did not use to ask them about that." Then they sent me to Abdur Rahman bin Abza and I asked him. He replied, "The companions of the Prophet used to practise Salam in the life-time of the Prophet; and we did not use to ask them whether they had standing crops or not."[6]

حَدَّثَنَا مُحَمَّدُ بْنُ أَبِي الْمُجَالِدِ قَالَ بَعَثَنِي عَبْدُ اللَّهِ بْنُ شَدَّادٍ وَأَبُو بُرْدَةَ إِلَى عَبْدِ اللَّهِ بْنِ أَبِي أَوْفَى رَضِيَ اللَّهُ عَنْهُمَا فَقَالَا سَلْهُ هَلْ كَانَ
أَصْحَابُ النَّبِيِّ صَلَّى اللَّهُ عَلَيْهِ وَسَلَّمَ فِي عَهْدِ النَّبِيِّ صَلَّى اللَّهُ عَلَيْهِ وَسَلَّمَ يُسْلِفُونَ فِي الْحِنْطَةِ قَالَ عَبْدُ اللَّهِ كُنَّا نُسْلِفُ نَبِيطَ أَهْلِ
الشَّأْمِ فِي الْحِنْطَةِ وَالشَّعِيرِ وَالزَّيْتِ فِي كَيْلٍ مَعْلُومٍ إِلَى أَجَلٍ مَعْلُومٍ قُلْتُ إِلَى مَنْ كَانَ أَصْلُهُ عِنْدَهُ قَالَ مَا كُنَّا نَسْأَلُهُمْ عَنْ ذَلِكَ ثُمَّ
بَعَثَانِي إِلَى عَبْدِ الرَّحْمَنِ بْنِ أَبْزَى فَسَأَلْتُهُ فَقَالَ كَانَ أَصْحَابُ النَّبِيِّ صَلَّى اللَّهُ عَلَيْهِ وَسَلَّمَ يُسْلِفُونَ عَلَى عَهْدِ النَّبِيِّ صَلَّى اللَّهُ عَلَيْهِ
وَسَلَّمَ وَلَمْ نَسْأَلْهُمْ أَلَهُمْ حَرْثٌ أَمْ لَا

According to Ibn Abas (mAbpwt), the *Qur'anic* verse 2:282 also refers to *salam*. He argues that since postponement of payment in a sale contract is allowed, then, by analogy, postponement of the delivery of the sold item can also be allowed. *Dayn* in verse 2: 282 refers to a deferred undertaking, whereas *salam* is also a deferred undertaking to deliver a specified amount of a well-defined commodity at a future specified date.[7]

Conditions for *salam* include:

- The price of the commodity must be known. Prices may fluctuate and the resulting uncertainty may cause injustice to one of the parties. Both parties, therefore, have to rely on a fixed price. *Salam* provides a hedge to the seller if the market price of the commodity goes down and a hedge to the purchaser if the market price goes up.
- The purchaser should pay the price of the *salam* commodity during the session of the contract, and the seller should possess the price. The purchaser is not allowed to defer the price or to consider his debt on the seller as the price of the *salam* commodity. Deferment of price will amount to the prohibited exchange of one obligation (*dayn*) for another obligation (*dayn*), because the *salam* commodity itself is an obligation or liability of the seller. Furthermore, the purpose of a *salam* contract is to provide farmers with funds they may need to finance their farming activities. It is an alternative to the interest-based loan and at the same time enables the farmers to sell their commodity. Advance payment of the price minimises the possibilities of default from both parties and strengthens the *salam* contract. The Maliki school, however, allows postponement of the payment of the price up to three days.[8]
- The sold commodity should be as an obligation (*dayn*) on the seller. *Salam* involves commodities that are not specific (*'ain*) but generic or homogeneous. It is not permitted to specify the fruits of a certain number of fruit trees or the crop of a certain acreage of sown field or farm.[9] For instance, it is permissible to sell 100 kg of grade A rice for RM 500 to be delivered at a specified future date. However, it is not permissible to sell 100 kg of rice that will be harvested from a specific acreage of land.
- The commodity should be described precisely by type, quantity, and quality.
- The seller should be able to deliver the commodity on the specified date.
- The place of delivery should be adequately specified.
- The price and the commodity should not belong to the same group of *ribawi* commodities.
- The type of the commodity on which *salam* is concluded must be readily available in the market. The condition is aimed to minimise the risk of nondelivery for cases in which the seller is not able to deliver the specified amount due to bad harvest. In such cases, the seller can source the commodity from the market. The Hanafis argue that the commodity should be available in the market from the time the *salam* contract is concluded until the

FIGURE 2.4 B can take possession of the rice only on November 1, when delivery is made. B cannot sell the rice to C prior to November 1, as he does not possess the rice.

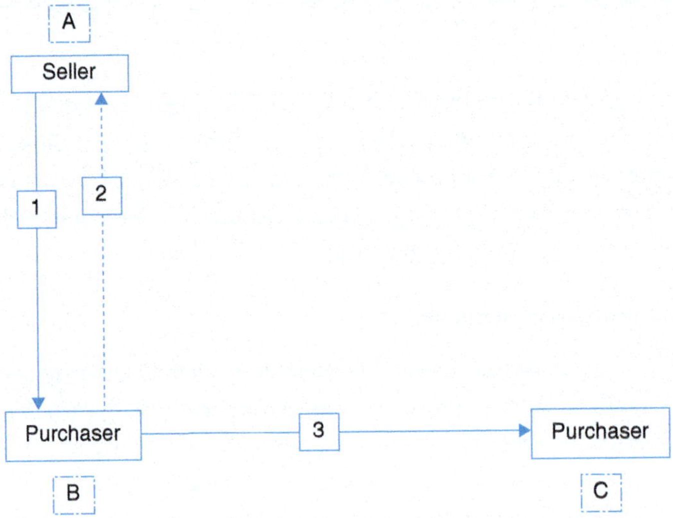

1. A sells 5 tons of rice to B through a *salam* contract on July 1. The rice will be delivered on November 1.
2. B pays the price on July 1.
3. B cannot sell the rice to C before November 1.

delivery is made. The majority of the *Fiqh* schools are of the opinion that it is sufficient that the commodity should be available in the market during the time of the delivery.

- The purchaser has the right to ask the seller to provide a guarantee or a pledge.
- The purchaser cannot dispose of the *salam* commodity by reselling it to a third person prior to its possession. The jurists are in agreement that it is not permissible. Figure 2.4 shows the concept. The *hadith* of the Prophet (pbAbuh) states: "Whoever buys foodstuff, he should not sell it (to others) until he has taken possession of them."[10]

عَنْ ابْنِ عَبَّاسٍ قَالَقَالَ رَسُولُ اللَّهِ صَلَّى اللَّهُ عَلَيْهِ وَسَلَّمَ مَنْ ابْتَاعَ طَعَامًا فَلَا يَبِعْهُ حَتَّى يَقْبِضَهُ
قَالَ ابْنُ عَبَّاسٍ وَأَحْسِبُ كُلَّ شَيْءٍ بِمَنْزِلَةِ الطَّعَامِ

There are two risks for a purchaser in a *salam* contract. First, the seller may fail to deliver the commodity, possibly due to force de majeure or circumstances beyond his control such as crop failure. Second, there is a price risk of the commodity, as the purchaser may find that, at the delivery date, the market price has fallen below that paid to the seller. In order to mitigate the first risk, the purchaser is entitled to require collateral. To mitigate the price risk, the purchaser may enter into a parallel *salam* contract under which he would sell a known quantity and quality of a commodity to a third party with the same or different delivery date as with the first *salam*

FIGURE 2.5 It is possible for B to sell the rice through another *salam* contract to C, where C pays the price on the spot. Note that the same rice cannot be sold through a normal sale in which the price is paid later.

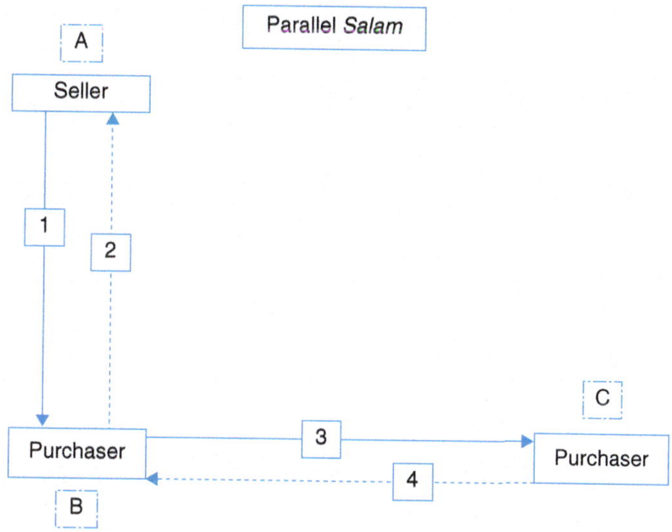

1. A sells 5 tons of a defined quality of rice to B through a *salam* contract on July 1. The rice will be delivered on November 1.
2. B pays the price on July 1.
3. B sells a known quantity of rice through a *salam* contract to C on August 1 to be delivered on November 1.
4. C pays the price upon the conclusion of contract on August 1.

contract and receive its price on the spot as required by the *salam* contract. However, the second *salam* contract should be separate from the first *salam* contract and should not depend on it. The structure of parallel *salam* appears in Figure 2.5.

Manufacturing Sale (*Bay'al-Istisna'*)

Istisna' is a contract with a seller who provides both raw materials and labour to manufacture a specifically defined product for a known price and deliver it at a specified date. The contract structure is presented in Figure 2.6. *Istisna'* is a unique sale contract that has its own specific features that distinguishes it from other sale contracts. The Hanafii jurists have argued on the basis of juristic preference (*istihsan*) that *istisna'* is a valid sale contract. They consider *istisna'* as a separate and independent contract in its own right that has its own unique features. The Hanafi scholars differentiate between *istisna'* and *salam* on the ground that *istisna'* contract involves both raw materials and labour, whereas *salam* is applicable to commodities only. They further argue that *istisna'* is a contract that involves the making or manufacturing of a specific thing (*'ain*), whereas the seller in *salam* is undertaking to deliver a generic/fungible commodity (*dayn*).

FIGURE 2.6 A manufacturer or a developer sells machinery to be manufactured or a house to be built to a purchaser. The price could be paid in advance, postponed, or by instalments.

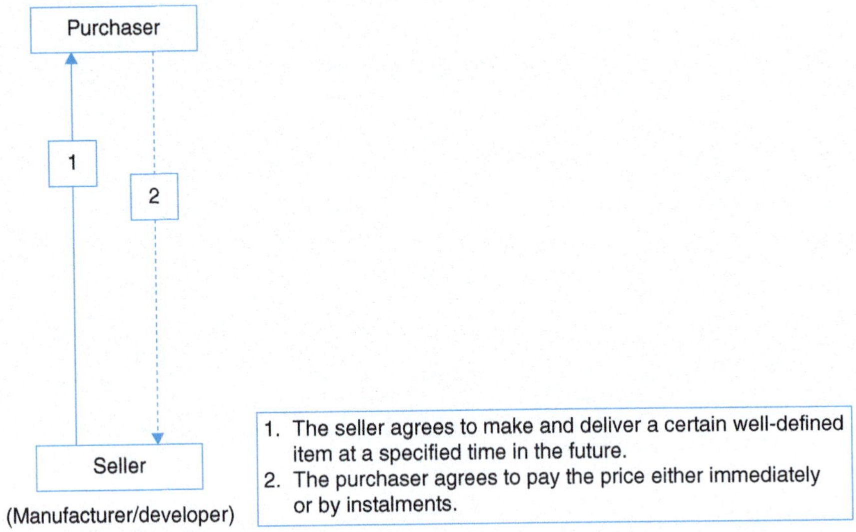

Conditions of *istisna'* include:

- The item to be manufactured should be described precisely. The nature, type, quality, quantity, and all other descriptions of the item to be manufactured should be known.
- *Istisna'* is valid in respect of those goods that are customarily sold based on a prior order. In other words, the item is such that requires time to be made and the common practice of the society acknowledges this.
- Date of delivery of the manufactured asset should be specified in the contract. This can also include the dates for the completion of the various stages in the constructions of manufactured items or buildings.
- The manufacturing process and other details should be specified in the contract.
- *Istisna'* contract is a binding contract on the parties, the seller/manufacturer, and the buyer. This means that a party cannot cancel the contract unilaterally and is obliged to fulfil its obligation at all times. Article 293 of the Mejjelle states: "After *Istisna'* is concluded by an agreement, the parties cannot go back on the bargain. But if the thing does not agree with the description, the person who gives the order has an option."
- It is permissible for the parties to include a penalty clause stipulating that a party who does not fulfil his contractual obligation should be penalised.[11] *Ahadith* of the Prophet (pbAbuh) states that "Muslims are bound by their conditions." Penalty refers to a sum payable by a party who delays his contractual obligation or fails to complete it. Damages are granted usually in proportion to the harm caused by the breach of the contract by one of the parties. Experts would determine the amount of damages in the light of justice, fairness, and equity as commanded by the *Shariah.* Fine and penalties can also be imposed to secure performance of

contract by a party. Unforeseen events or events that cannot be avoided are excluded from the application of this condition.

- Payment of the entire price of the manufactured item could be deferred to a future date or paid by instalments within a fixed and known duration.

Options of Istisna'

The two most important options that could be exercised in *istisna'* are the option of defect and the option of desired description. The option of desired description refers to the right of the buyer to rescind the contract due to the absence and violation of the description stipulated by the contracting parties for the subject matter of the contract. The option must be stipulated. For example, the customer ordered a red car and the supplier delivered a blue one. The buyer has two choices. He may return the goods or he may take them in full price, because the violation of a description may not necessarily affect the price.

Islamic Banks and Istisna' *Contracts*

In *istisna'* it is not necessary that the seller himself should manufacture the item. He can fulfil his obligation by delivering the sold item with an exact prescribed description that is manufactured by a third party. The buyer, however, may stipulate that the item should be made from specific materials or made by a particular manufacturer or a particular construction company. This may enable Islamic banks to enter into *istisna'* contracts with a customer and a manufacturer/developer simultaneously. The structure for parallel *istisna'* is presented in Figure 2.7. An Islamic bank may first enter into an *istisna'* contract with a customer and sell to him a specified house that is under construction or a car to be manufactured. The bank next will enter into a parallel *istisna'* contract with a developer or a manufacturer as the case may be. The payment in both *istisna'* contracts can be immediate or deferred. The bank would have to sign two separate contracts, one with the seller and the other with the customer. Any disagreements that may arise between the parties are settled under each contract separately.

The differences between *istisna'* and other sale contracts include the following:

- *Istisna'* is distinguished from the ordinary sale contract by the fact that the former involves labour, whereas the latter does not. Furthermore, in *istisna'* a nonexistent thing that will be manufactured or produced later is sold, whereas in an ordinary sale a nonexistent thing cannot be sold.
- *Istisna'* is different from a *murabahah* sale because *murabahah* is a trust sale in which the cost price and the profit should be known to the purchaser, whereas in *istisna'*, the price is determined based on the agreement between the parties.
- According to the Hanafiis, *istisna'* is distinguished from a *salam* sale on the grounds that the commodity in *salam* is generic and, therefore, an obligation (*dayn*) on the seller, whereas in *istisna'*, a certain specific thing (*'ain*) is sold to the purchaser. Moreover, in a *salam* sale, the

FIGURE 2.7 The bank has entered into two *istisna'* contracts, one with the purchaser (customer), in which the bank acts as a seller, and the other with the seller (manufacturer or developer), in which the bank acts as a purchaser.

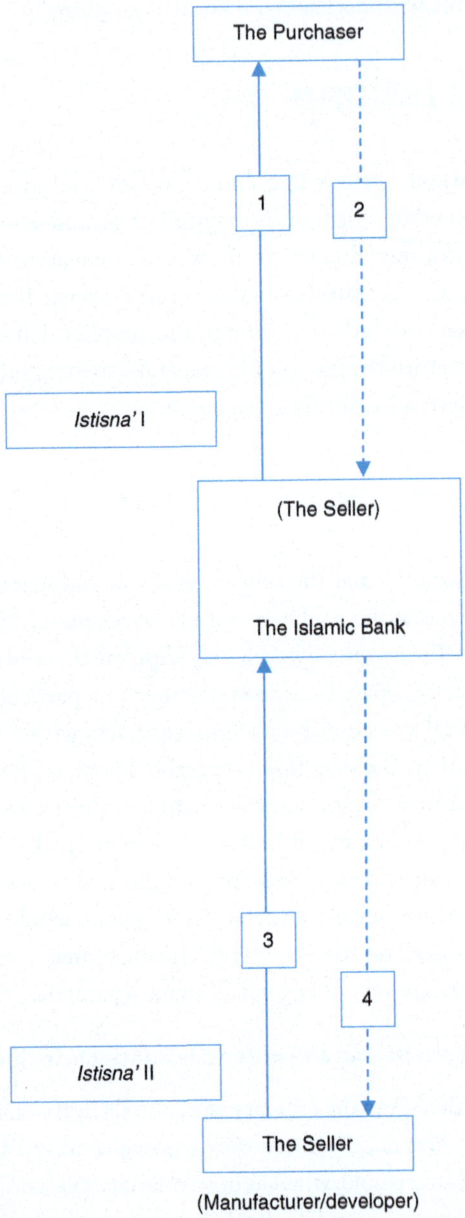

1. The seller (Islamic Bank) agrees to deliver a certain well-defined item at a specific time in the future.
2. The purchaser agrees to pay the price by instalments.
3. The seller (manufacturer/developer) agrees to make and deliver the same well-defined item at the same specified time as agreed in no. 2.
4. The purchaser (Islamic Bank) agrees to pay the price either immediately or based on the various manufacturing/development phases.

price is paid upon signing the contract, whereas in *istisna'*, the price may be paid in advance, by instalments, or deferred to a future date.

- *Istisna'* is also distinguished from the employment (*ijarah*) contract by the fact that, in *istisna'*, the maker/manufacturer provides both the raw materials and the labour, whereas in *ijarah*, a person provides raw materials, and a maker/manufacturer as an employee contributes his labour and skill to make the required item.

Currency Exchange (*Bay' al-Sarf*)

Currency exchange (*al-sarf*) is defined as the sale or exchange of a price for a price in the same or different currency, and each price is a consideration for the other, as shown in Figure 2.8. For instance, a dinar or gold could be exchanged for dinar or a dinar for dirham. Historically gold and silver were used as moneys and as references for defining prices. Although they are stores of wealth, as they have their own intrinsic value, they can also become a medium of exchange and units of accounting. Money (*thaman*) is not a commodity but a medium of exchange and a price for goods and commodities. The main function of the money is to be used for pricing different properties. Money, therefore, must provide a stable universal reference for defining prices. Its value should not increase or decrease but should always remain stable. Muslim jurists have considered gold and silver as prices (*thaman*) and treated them differently from other commodities. Later, however, fiat money or paper currencies were introduced, which replaced gold and silver. The contract of *sarf*, which was applicable to golden dinar and silver dirham, is also equally applicable to fiat money.

FIGURE 2.8 A person sells a known amount of Ringgit for a known amount of Euros. Both currencies are exchanged on the spot.

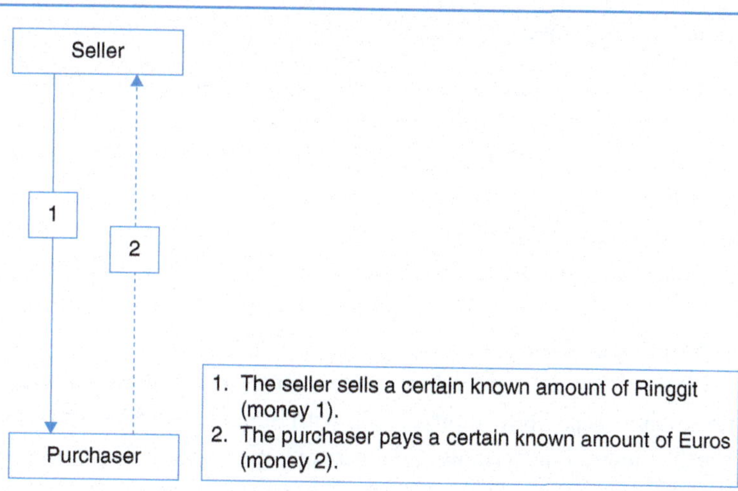

Money should not be bought and sold like commodities and goods. If money is treated as a commodity, it will have a price that may fluctuate from time to time. It will be sold and purchased for profit. This will change the role of money as a medium of exchange to a mere commodity. Indeed, the very use of money as a commodity for profit is the essence of usury (*riba*). Interest/usury has effectively turned currencies into commodities. It would also turn the money, which is only a means, into an end in itself. Fluctuations in the price of money will attract currency speculators. Instead of using the money for useful investment and productive purposes it will be sold and purchased for speculative purposes.

Islamic law has therefore provided a special sale contract of *sarf* for the exchange of currencies and provided strict conditions for its validity. The *hadith* on *riba al-fadhl* that stipulates the equality of counter-values and spontaneity of exchange is also applicable to currency exchange. The Hadith states:

> Abu Sa'id al-Khudri (May Allah be pleased with him) reported Allah's Messenger (pbAbuh) as saying: Gold is to be paid for by gold, silver by silver, wheat by wheat, barley by barley, dates by dates, salt by salt, like by like, payment being made hand to hand. He who made an addition to it, or asked for an addition, in fact dealt in usury. The receiver and the giver are equally guilty.[12]

لذَّهَبِوَالْفِضَّةُبِالْفِضَّةِوَالْبُرُّبِالْبُرِّوَالشَّعِيرُبِالشَّعِيرِوَالتَّمْرُبِالتَّمْرِوَالْمِلْحُبِالْمِلْحِمِثْلاًبِمِثْلٍيَدًابِيَدٍفَمَنْزَادَأَوِاسْتَزَادَفَقَدْأَرْبَىالآخِذُ
وَالْمُعْطِيفِيهِسَوَاءٌ الذَّهَبُا

Fluctuations in the price of money will attract currency speculators. Instead of using the money for useful investment and productive purposes it will be sold and purchased for speculative purposes.

Conditions for *sarf* include:

- The parties should take mutual possession of the prices during the session of the contract before their separation. If the parties do not take possession of the moneys they exchange, the contract in substance is the exchange of one obligation for another (*bay' al-kali bil-kali*), which amounts to usury (*riba*) and is prohibited.
- There should not be any deferment in the exchange of one of the currencies. The principle concerning money is that it cannot be sold or bought on credit but should be exchanged on the spot. It follows from this that money can only be exchanged on a cash basis. The sale of price for price, gold for gold, or silver for silver on credit is prohibited by the *hadith* on *Riba al-fadhl*. A party who does not deliver his countervalue but takes possession of the other party's countervalue keeps both countervalues with him. He deprives the other person of his right to use the money. Furthermore, if delivery of both countervalues is not done on the spot, this

may encourage the parties to breach the contract for cases in which the current exchange rate does not favor them. Speculation is only possible when currencies are traded for future.

- Fixing the price but postponing the delivery of one of the prices may amount to imposing a current price on the future currencies market. If one currency is delivered and the other currency is not, the contract in substance is *qardh* and not *sarf*. In this case, the same amount in the same currency should be returned to the lender.
- When both the moneys exchanged are of the same kind, then equality is also necessary. Unequal exchange of gold for silver and vice versa is allowed provided it is on the spot.
- The currency exchange contract is binding. The only option available in a *sarf* transaction is the option of defect.

Chapter Questions

True/False

1. ( ) In a bargain (*musawamah*) sale certain goods are sold based on their cost price with an added profit.
2. ( ) In a *murabaha* contract, the Islamic bank is acting as an agent who purchases the property on behalf of the customer.
3. ( ) In a *salam* contract, a purchaser can sell the *salam* commodity to others before he acquires the commodity.
4. ( ) In a *salam* contract, it is not permissible for the seller to sell certain crops in a specific field.
5. ( ) The parties in a *salam* contract may agree that the price should be determined when the commodity is actually delivered.
6. ( ) The purchaser in a *salam* contract can pay earnest money (*'urbun*) on the spot and defer the balance to a later time.
7. ( ) In a *salam* contract, the commodity sold is considered an obligation (*dayn*) on the seller.
8. ( ) In a *salam* contract, the purchaser can ask for collateral from the seller.
9. ( ) In an *istisna'* contract, both the raw materials and labour should be provided by the seller.
10. ( ) In an *istisna'* contract, a purchaser employs a seller to make for him a certain well-defined and known item.
11. ( ) In an *istisna'* sale, the payment of the price can be postponed to a future date.
12. ( ) In an *istisna'* contract, raw materials are provided by one party and labour, workmanship, or expertise by another.
13. ( ) The unequal sale of Ringgit for Euro, on credit is allowed because they belong to two different types of currencies.
14. ( ) In a sale of currencies, both currencies should be exchanged on the spot.
15. ( ) In an exchange of currencies, both currencies should be in cash and present.

Short Answer

1. Discuss how *istisna'* is distinguished from the contracts of ordinary sale, employment (*ijarah*), and *salam*.
2. Explain how Islamic banks may apply the contract of *istisna'*.
3. Briefly discuss the conditions for a valid transaction of *sarf*.
4. If the deferred price of a house is higher than its cash price, it may amount to usury (*riba*) because the increase in the price is due to the time factor. Do you agree that the cash and deferred price of a house should remain the same? Provide reasons for your agreement or disagreement.

Notes

1. Yusuf al-Qaradawi, *The Lawful and the Prohibited in Islam* (Kuala Lumpur: Islamic Book Trust, 1995), 269–270.
2. Muhammad Taqi Usmani, *An Introduction to Islamic Finance* (Karachi: Maktaba Ma'ariful Qur'an, 2004), 115.
3. Ibid, 116.
4. See Islamic Fiqh Academy, Resolution No. 2 and No. 3; see also *Journal of the Islamic Fiqh Academy* 2, no. 5:1509, M. Tahir Mansuri. *Islamic Law of Contracts and Business Transactions* (Islamabad: Shari'ah Academy, International Islamic University Islamabad 2001), 217.
5. M. Muhsin Khan, *Sahih-al-Bukhari*, vol.3, book 35, no. 2240 (Riyadh: Darussalam, 1997).
6. Ibid, Hadith number 2244.
7. See as-Sayyid Sabiq, *Fiqh as-Sunnah* (Cairo: Dar al-Hadith, 2004), 926.
8. See Wahbah al-Zuhaili, *Financial Transactions in Islamic Jurisprudence*, vol.1, 241–242.
9. See Yusuf al-Qaradawi, *The Lawful and the Prohibited in Islam*, trans. Kamal El-Helbawy (Kuala Lumpur: Islamic Book Trust, 1995), 270.
10. *Sahih Muslim*, chapter 8, on the invalidity to sell a commodity before taking its possession, p. 68, Hadith no. 2808.
11. See The OIC Fiqh Academy, seventh session, item 67/3/7 – no. 4.
12. Abdul Hamid Siddiqui, *Translation of Sahih Muslim*, book 10, Hadith no. 3854 (Beirut: Dar al-'Arabiyah, 1972).

CHAPTER

3

The Contracts of Employment and Lease (*Ijarah*), Borrowing (*I'arah*), and Reward (*Ja'alah*)

Learning outcomes

At the end of this chapter, you should be able to:

1. Define and understand the contracts of *ijarah*, *i'arah,* and *ja'alah.*
2. Identify the main constituent pillars and important conditions of these contracts.
3. Understand the various types of *ijarah* contracts and their different uses.
4. Compare and contrast the *ijarah* contract with the *i'arah* and *ja'alah* contracts.

Introduction

The word *ijarah* is derived from the root word *ajr,* which means compensation. Legally, *ijarah* is defined as a sale of usufruct or service in return for compensation. Although *ijarah* is the sale of usufruct, it is distinguished from a sale by the fact that *ijarah,* unlike sale, is for a limited time. Moreover, in a lease contract the possession of the leased asset is transferred to the lessee, whereas the lessor retains ownership of the asset. The subject matter of the *ijarah* contract is the usufruct of an asset or the service that is rendered by an employee. Usufruct (*manfa'ah*) refers to abstract and intangible benefit that is derived from a certain property such as the shelter from a house or a lift from a horse or car, or service rendered by an employee. Usufruct is derived from usable properties, whereas service, which also comes under the category of usufruct, is rendered by persons who are employed to do a certain well-defined job. Things that, if used, could be consumed cannot be leased. For instance fruit, food, or money cannot be leased because they are consumed when used. Although usufruct or service is nonexistent at the time that *ijarah* is concluded, it gradually comes into existence through the tenure of the contract.

Things that, if used, could be consumed cannot be leased. For instance fruit, food, or money cannot be leased because they are consumed when used.

The followings are the verses of the *Qur'an* and *Hadith* on *ijarah* contract.

Is it they who would portion out the mercy of thy Lord? It is we who portion out between them their livelihood in the life of this world: and we raise some of them above others in ranks, so that some may command work from others. But the mercy of thy Lord is better than the (wealth) which they amass.

The Qur'an 43: 32

أهم يقسمون رحمت ربك نحن قسمنا بينهم معيشتهم في الحياة الدنيا و رفعنا بعضهم فوق بعض درجات ليتخذ بعضهم بعضا سخريا ورحمت ربك خير مما يجمعون

If you decide on a foster-mother for your off spring there is no blame on you, provided you pay (the mother) what you offered, on equitable terms.

The Qur'an 2: 233

و إن أردتم أن تسترضعوا أولادكم فلا جناح عليكم إذا سلمتم ما اتيتم بالمعروف

And if they suckle your (offspring) give them their recompense.

The Qur'an 65: 6

فإن أرضعن لكم فأتوهن أجورهن

Afterwards one of the (damsels) came (back) to him, walking bashfully. She said: "My father invites thee that he may reward thee for having watered (our flocks) for us."

The Qur'an 28: 25

فجاءته إحداهما تمشى على استحياء قالت إن أبي يدعوك ليجزيك أجر ما سقيت لنا

Said one of the (damsels): O, my (dear) father; engage him on wages: truly the best of men for thee to employ is the (man) who is strong and trusty.

The Qur'an 28: 26

قالت إحداهما يا أبت استأجره إن خير من استأجرت القوي الأمين

A *Hadith* of the Prophet (pbAbuh) states: "Give an employee his wage before his sweat dries up."[1]

أعطوا الأجير أجره قبل أن يجف عرقه

The Pillars of the *Ijarah* Contract

The Hanafii jurists argue that the contract of *ijarah* has two pillars of offer and acceptance. However, according to the majority of the *Fiqh* schools *ijarah* has four pillars. They are:

1. Expression, which includes both offer and acceptance.
2. The parties, who include both the lessor and the lessee or the employer and the employee.
3. Wage/salary/rent.
4. Usufruct, service.

The Types of Ijarah *Contract*

The contract of *ijarah* could generally be divided into two contracts of lease and employment. In the following pages, we will discuss each type of *ijarah* contract separately and its terms and conditions.

The Contract of Employment

Employment is of two types: The first is a special employee (*al-ajeer al-khas*) who works for one employer for a specific wage, as shown in Figure 3.1. He is employed for a known period and a well-defined service. During the period of the contract, he is not allowed to work for another employer. He is completely subject to the control of his employer in terms of what he does and now he does it.

FIGURE 3.1 An employee provides a service to the employer in return for a wage/salary.

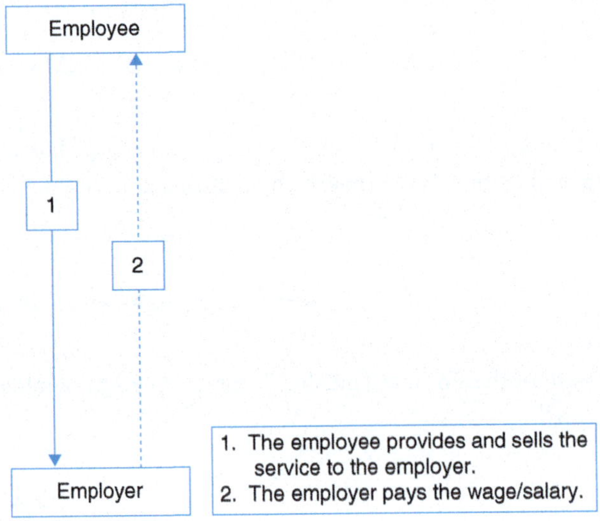

The public or general employee (*al-ajeer al-'aam*) or an independent contractor, on the other hand, is his own master and works for himself. A tailor, a carpenter, a shoemaker, a butcher, a physician, a dentist, or a consultancy firm is an example of general employee. They may work for more than one employer as presented in Figure 3.2. An employer cannot stop them from working for others. However, a general employee must provide the service or work which he has undertaken, though he can determine his own method of performance insofar as the terms of his contract permit. A general employee is entitled to payment based on his work. General employee needs many customers/employers in order to run his business.

Conditions for the service/labour (*manfa'ah*) include:

- The type of work or job to be performed and the service should be known and clearly defined. The duration of employment should also be clearly mentioned. This is to avoid ambiguity and the resulting conflicts.
- The service should be permissible and be used for lawful purposes. For instance employment in *haram* industries is not allowed.
- The service should not be obligatory on the person who rendered it. A person should not be paid for a service that is obligatory on him to render. Consequently, *ijarah* is not valid if made with a person who is under obligation to render a certain service. For instance, a wife cannot demand wages for doing household jobs or for breast-feeding the child. However, it is permissible to employ a wet nurse to breast-feed and provide care to the child, but not the child's mother if she is not divorced. Similarly, a person who is employed and being paid to render certain services to the public cannot ask the people to pay him or her for rendering the same service to them because this amounts to bribery and corruption.

FIGURE 3.2 A consultancy firm provides services to different companies and charges them fees.

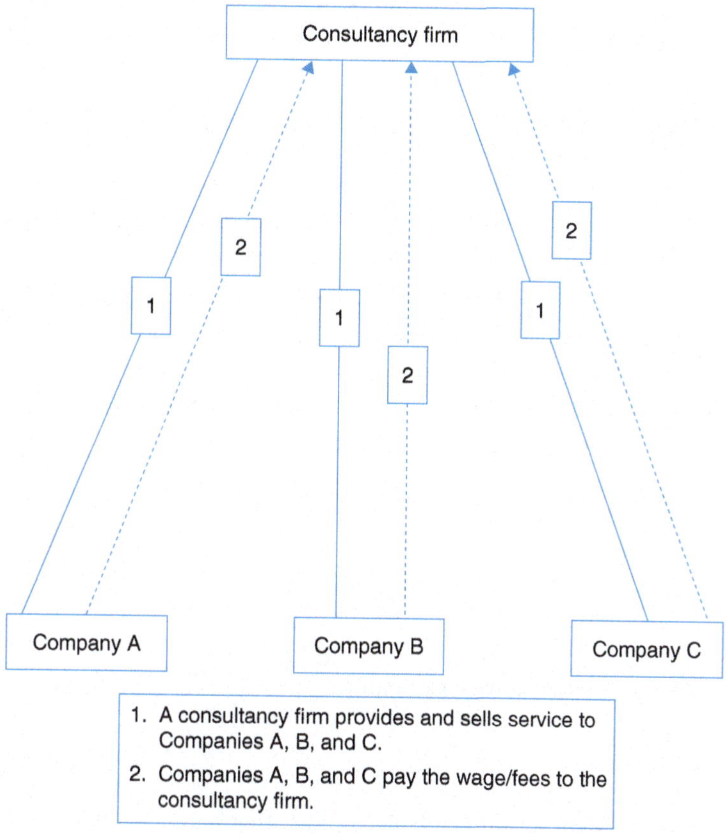

- The service rendered by an employee should not be of benefit to the employee. If an employee benefits from the service he renders, the contract does not fall under employment. *Ijarah* is not possible when an employee has his own interest in the work done. For instance, it is not permissible to employ a person to grind a certain measure of wheat that the employee jointly owns with the employer. In this case the employee benefits from his work and is working for himself.[2] Based on this principle, a partner may not be employed by other partners for running and managing the partnership business. Such a partner-employee becomes an employee for himself because he is also a partner in the same partnership. He, however, may receive a higher percentage in the profit compared to other partners who do not contribute to the management. Similarly, graduating students who need to do their internship or practical training with companies are not considered employees of the companies and are not paid as working in companies meant for their benefit to help them gain experience.
- The wage or salary should be declared to the employee and known clearly in the contract. The Hadith of the Prophet (pbAbuh) states: "Anyone who employs an employee should make known to him his wage."[3]

من استأجر أجيرا فليعلمه أجره

The payment could be made in advance, paid periodically such as weekly or monthly, or postponed to the end of the employment period. If there are no conditions about the mode of payment, and if the employment contract is for a certain period, it is then necessary to pay at the end of that period. If the employment is for a certain work, the payment should be made when the work is done.

- The majority of the *Fiqh* schools are of the opinion that the contract of employment (*ijarah*) is void if a person is employed on the condition that he would receive as his wage a certain percentage of the income from his work or a certain percentage of the produce of the work that he performs—for example, when a person is employed to pick fruit on the condition that he would be paid in fruit. He may not need the fruit and has to sell it for a lower price. Similarly, it is not allowed if an owner of a taxi employs a driver for a wage of RM 100 to be paid from the income of the taxi. It is void because there is the possibility that there may not be enough earning on a particular day as a result of which the driver may be paid less or not paid at all. These schools rely on the Hadith of the Prophet (pbAbuh) in which he has prohibited the hiring of a worker to grind wheat with his wages paid in flour."

نهى رسول الله صلى الله عليه و سلم عن قفيز الطحان

The Hanafiis have derived a general principle from this Hadith. The principle is this: Any condition that the wages should be paid from the income of the work that the employee performs makes *ijarah* contract voidable.

القاعدة: تعين الأجر مما يعمل فيه الأجير مفسد للعقد

The Malikis, and Hanbalis, on the other hand, argue for the permissibility of paying an employee from the proceeds of his work provided the in-kind payment is known. They do not consider this Hadith as authentic (*sahih*).[4]

The Contract of Lease/Rent

A lease contract could be used for movable assets such as cars, or for immovable assets such as houses and buildings, as shown in Figure 3.3. There are at least three reasons why people lease properties. They may need the asset for a short duration or the asset could be too expensive and a person may not be able to afford it. Sometimes there could be the combination of both reasons—the asset is too expensive and it is needed for a short duration.

Conditions for the usufruct:

- The leased property must be owned by the lessor. It is not permitted to lease an asset that is not owned by the lessor.
- The leased asset and the usufruct (*manfa'ah*) should be known. This is possible when the leased and the usufruct are clearly defined and the duration of the lease contract is clearly mentioned. This is to avoid ambiguity and the resulting conflicts.

FIGURE 3.3 A person leases his house or car to a lessee in return for a rental.

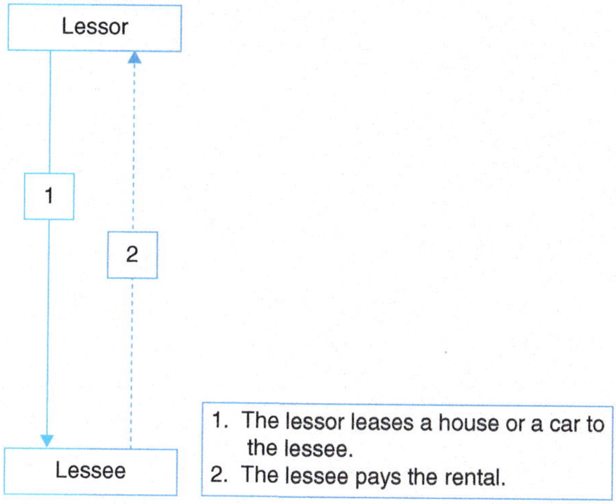

- Because it is impossible to deliver the usufruct (*manfa'ah*), the asset from which the usufruct is derived should be delivered. Although the ownership of the leased asset remains with the lessor, the possession should be transferred to the lessee.
- The usufruct should be attainable. It is not allowed to rent money or perishable properties from which usufruct cannot be obtained. Similarly, a house that is not suitable for living or a car that cannot be driven cannot be rented because it is not possible to derive any benefit or usufruct from these properties.
- The leased asset should be a permissible and valuable (*mutaqawwim*) property. For instance, the leased asset should not be a stolen car, slot machine for gambling, or vats for producing alcoholic beverages. The usufruct should also be used for permissible purposes. It is also not allowed to rent a house for gambling.
- The usufruct should be used for the same purpose for which the asset is rented. The usufruct could also be shared among a number of lessees provided the asset is used for the same purpose.

Maintenance of the Leased Asset

The lessor has to bear the risk of undeliberate loss or destruction of the asset. He also has to bear the risk of depreciation of the leased asset, and payment of taxes and insurance, whereas the lessee should bear the cost related to current expenditure that may be necessary for utilising the asset during the leasing period. If the leased asset is not in good working conditions and has a defect, the lessee has the option to cancel the contract or to continue with it. At the end of the lease period, the lessee is under obligation to return the asset to the owner.

There is no liability on a lessee, employee, or tenant, except when it is established that he has transgressed or wasted and damaged the leased property. In such a case, the lessee, employee, or tenant is liable to repair or replace the property.

Sale of the Leased Asset

The leasing contract is considered binding and irrevocable. The lessee may sell the leased asset provided the purchaser knows and agrees to the continuity of the lease contract. All terms and conditions, rights, and liabilities agreed upon in the lease contract will be transferred to the new owner. The lease contract, however, will continue until its stipulated time. If the purchaser is not aware of the lease, he has the right to rescind the contract.

Can an Orchard Be Leased for Its Fruit?

Renting an orchard for its fruit is not allowed, because fruits could not be classified as usufruct because they are tangible things. Besides being an invalid lease contract, the lease of orchard for fruit also involves *gharar.* The amount of fruit may be more or less the amount of rental paid. If the price of the fruit harvested is more than the rental paid, the owner of the orchard will suffer losses. However, if the price of the fruit is lower or the amount of the fruit collected is less, then the lessee would suffer. Furthermore, the quality cannot be guaranteed because some of the fruits may be affected by disease or may be rotten, and in such cases the lessor would suffer. In form, the contract is an invalid lease, but in substance it is an invalid sale contract, due to the existence of *gharar,* because the amount and quality of the fruit is not known. A more preferable contract in such cases is *salam,* in which a known amount of fruit is sold for a known price. Thus, instead of leasing an orchard for fruit, the fruit should be sold for a known weight at a known price.

Islamic Banks and Leases

The banks or leasing companies use two models of lease contract. They are Operational Lease and Lease, Then Purchase.

Operational Lease

Operational lease refers to an ordinary lease or rent (*ijarah*) contract. It is suitable for those assets that are expensive and their purchase requires a great amount of money or those assets that take a long time to manufacture. It is also suitable for those assets that are needed for a short period of time. Because of these factors, there is increasing demand for leasing these assets. The types of assets include aircrafts, ships, industrial equipment, agricultural machinery, cranes, and construction machinery. Other items may include Xerox machines, exercise machines, furniture, wedding gowns, and medical equipment such as therapeutic beds. A leasing company leases an asset to a lessee on terms and conditions agreed upon for a specific time. After the termination of the period, the asset is returned to the company. The company then leases the same asset to a new lessee. The leasing company bears the risk of depreciation of the asset or diminishing demand for these assets. At the end, the company may choose to scrap or dispose of the asset. A leasing company benefits from the transaction by retaining the ownership of the asset while it gets a return by leasing it. The lessee also benefits from the transaction because it meets his immediate need and saves him from buying the asset at a much higher cost and maintaining the asset. A lessee is not offered an option to buy the leased asset at the end of the lease period.

A normal lease is suitable for those assets that are expensive and are needed for a short period of time.

Lease, Then Purchase/Financial Lease

It refers to a type of lease (*ijarah*) contract in which the lessee has an option to purchase the leased asset at the end of the lease period. Unlike operational lease, the asset will not be returned to the lessor at the end of the lease period but will be bought by the lessee. The concept used by Islamic banks is referred to as *Al-Ijarah Thumma Al-Bai* (Aitab) or *Ijarah Muntahia Bittamleek*, which literally means "a lease then sale" and "a lease that ends with ownership of the lessee," respectively. It comprises two separate contracts: a contract of lease and a contract of sale at the end of the leasing period. Shari'ah Standard No. (9) of the Accounting and Auditing Organization for Islamic Financial Institutions states:

> It must be noted that the permissible *Ijarah Muntahia Bittamleek* is different from hire-purchase as commonly practised by conventional banks in the following respects. In hire-purchase the terms and provisions of sale and leasing are applied to the subject matter at the same time, and subsequently the ownership of the subject matter is transferred to the lessee (buyer), once he pays the last installment without the need for a separate contract for the transfer of ownership. In the permissible Ijarah Muntahia Bittamleek, on the other hand, the provisions governing ijarah are applied to the leased asset until the end of ijarah term, after which the lessee obtains ownership of the asset in the manner explained in this Standard.[5]

For example, a leasing company or a bank may purchase a vehicle based on a promise from a customer who undertakes to own it through lease. The bank will lease the vehicle for a specified period of time. The rental rates will be the calculated based on the value of the asset, its lifespan, its maintenance expenses, and some profit to the bank. The bank may ask for a deposit of one to two months in order to ensure the payment of rentals. If the lessee delays payment or fails to pay the rentals, the bank may cancel the lease contract after giving due notice to the lessee. The lessee is given the option to purchase the leased asset at the end of the lease period.

Because the asset is not yet sold, the bank should not pass on the ownership risk to the lessee. The bank owns the vehicle throughout the lease period and should take ownership risk. Insurance coverage should be borne by the lessor because of the possibility of theft or total loss due to accident. The bank will be paid by the insurer and the lessee will not gain anything except that he is no longer obliged to return the asset to the lessee. Nevertheless, the bank is entitled to compensation as a result of negligence by the lessee in maintaining the vehicle.

The lessee may purchase the vehicle during the lease period at a market price. If a lessee chooses to buy the asset during the lease period, the existing lease contract will be cancelled and a new sale contract will be concluded. All the lease rentals previously paid will constitute part of the price. For cases in which the customer no longer desires to continue with the lease arrangement, he may surrender or sell his right to another customer to continue with the lease and subsequently purchase the vehicle.

Termination of Ijarah

The contract of *ijarah* may come to an end in the following cases:

- If the asset is not capable of giving the usufruct.
- If the lessee or tenant fails to pay the rental or adhere to other conditions.
- If the leased asset is destroyed.
- According to the Hanafiis, a lease contract comes to an end if either of the parties dies. They argue that usufruct is not property, and, as such, it cannot be inherited by the heirs of the lessor in case the lessor dies. The majority of the *Fiqh* schools consider usufruct a form of property and argue that the *ijarah* contract should continue until its stipulated time. According to them, the right to stay can be inherited.
- By the mutual consent (*iqalah*) of the parties.
- Lapse of the agreed on time. For example, if the contract is for one year, it is terminated at the end of that period.

The Contract of Borrowing Things (*al-I'arah*)

According to the Hanafii and Maliki jurists, *i'arah* is a contract in which the usufruct of an asset is transferred to a borrower without compensation. According to these jurists, the borrower of the property temporarily and gratuitously owns the usufruct of that property. The Shafi'i and Hanbali jurists, on the other hand, define *i'arah* as a permission given by an owner to another to use a certain asset without compensation. These jurists are of the opinion that in *i'arah* permission is given to a borrower to use the property. This, they argue, does not mean that the ownership of the usufruct is transferred to him. Consequently, they view *i'arah* as a permission contract and not one that establishes the borrower's ownership of the usufruct. As a consequence of this disagreement over the definition of *i'arah*, the Hanafii and Maliki jurists argue that a borrower of an item may re-lend it to others, whereas the Shafi'i and Hanbali jurists do not permit this.[6] The contract is presented in Figure 3.4

The contract of *i'arah* is encouraged and recommended as a form of charitable deed. The property is held on trust by the borrower who is therefore not liable for its destruction, loss, or diminution of value, unless caused intentionally or by his fault and negligence. The borrower is held liable if the property is damaged due to misuse. The contract of *i'arah* has four pillars. They are lender (*al-mu'ir*), borrower (*al-musta'ir*), the borrowed item (*musta'ar*), and expression that includes offer and acceptance.

FIGURE 3.4 B borrows a book from A. B is under obligation to return the same book.

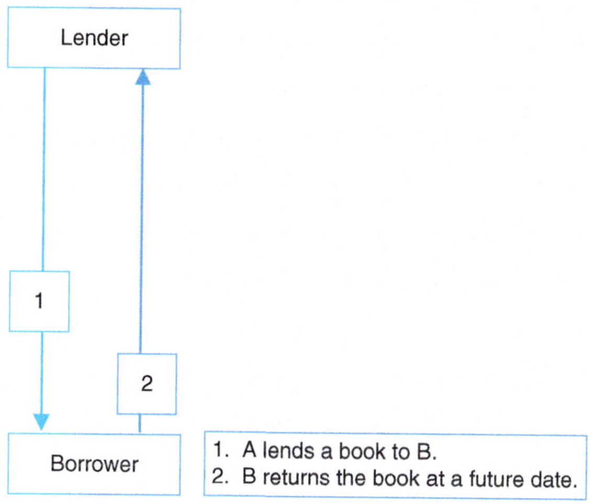

Important conditions for *i'arah:*

- The borrowed item should be known. It must be a usable property that is not consumed by its use.
- No condition is allowed that requires the return of any object other than the borrowed object.
- The borrower may lend the borrowed object to a third party, but he must not rent it out or give it as a pledge or security.
- The borrower of the item is bound to observe all conditions imposed by the lender about the usage of the item and the duration of its usage.
- The borrower is entitled to make use of the borrowed item without consideration or payment, but the borrower should meet the maintenance expenses of the property while it is in the borrower's possession and must return it at the termination of the *i'arah* contract.
- Both the lender and the borrower of the item may cancel the contract at any time.

The Contract of Reward for Service (*al-Ja'alah*)

Ja'alah is a binding promise to pay a certain reward to any person who performs a certain known task, as shown in Figure 3.5. The Malikis define *ja'alah* as a hiring or employment contract for a benefit that is possible to attain. The way *ja'alah* is defined shows differences of opinions about whether it is a binding promise or a unilateral contract. There are also differences of opinions among jurists on whether *ja'alah* is permitted or not. The Malikis permit *ja'alah* on the condition that there should not be any deadline for the completion of the task and that the amount

FIGURE 3.5 A offers a reward for the performance of a specific service. B provides the service and claims the reward.

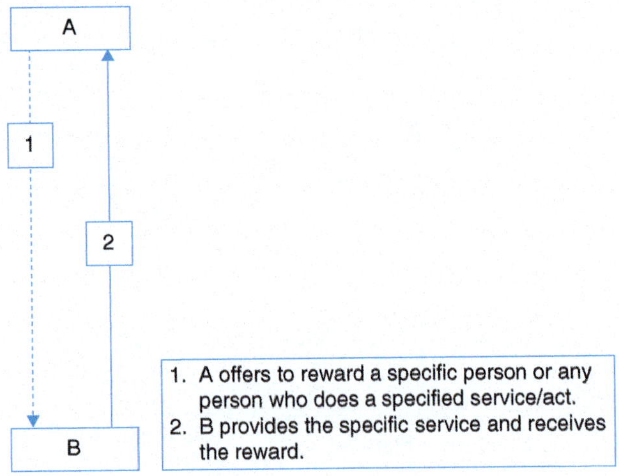

of reward should be known.[7] The Malikiis, Shafi'is, and Hanbaliis who argue for the validity of *ja'alah* rely on the *Qur'anic* verse that states, "They said 'we miss the great beaker of the king; for him who produces it, is (the reward of) a camel load; I will be bound by it'" (Qur'an: 12:72).

قالوا نفقد صواع الملك، ولمن جاء به حمل بعير، وأنا به زعيم

The Hanafiis, on the other hand, argue based on analogy with other employment (*ijarah*) contracts that *ja'alah* is not permitted because it suffers from ambiguity (*gharar*). They argue that in *ja'alah*, unlike *ijarah*, the amount of the service and the duration for the completion of the task are not known.

In *ja'alah,* one party undertakes to pay a specified amount of money for rendering a defined service in accordance with the terms and conditions declared. The person who offers a reward unilaterally binds himself to give a certain known payment for a certain known and specified action. For example, a person may make an offer that anyone who returns his lost horse or car will be rewarded RM 500, or a person may declare that he would pay RM 10,000 to anyone who develops a new software plan for his company. *Ja'alah* also includes rewards given to winners in a certain permissible competition or a reward declared for the discovery of a certain medicine for a disease or for any other useful scientific discoveries. The act sought must result from the efforts of the offeree, and should not be a mere gamble or the chance occurrence of certain events. For example, a person cannot promise a reward to another if a certain football team wins the competition, as the offeree does not make any efforts. However, such a reward could be offered to the team as a whole, as members of the team provide efforts.

In *ja'alah* the risk of nonperformance is shifted to the offeree or worker, since he earns nothing if the task is not completed. For instance, an offeree earns nothing if a lost property for which a reward is offered is not found. Hence, the task sought must be fully completed by the offeree. He is not entitled to the reward if the task is not completed.

Important conditions for *ja'alah*:

- Both the offerer (*ja'il*) and the offeree/doer (*'aamil*) should have complete legal capacity to become a party to a contract.
- An offer of reward could be made to a specific person or unknown person or persons.
- The amount of reward (*ja'al*) should be known at the time the offer is made. The amount of reward cannot be left uncertain or conditional on later events such as a percentage of the ultimate market value of goods recovered.
- The services offered by a doer should be permissible. As a general rule *ja'alah* is not valid for all those services for which employment (*ijarah*) is not valid.
- The reward must be a known permissible property, otherwise it is not valid.
- The Malikiis stipulate that there should not be a time limit in a *ja'alah* contract. The other jurists, however, are of the opinion that an offeror may set a deadline for the completion of the task.
- *Ja'alah* is not valid unless an offer is made by an offeror which would indicate his declaration or request for the performance of a certain action in return for a certain payment. If a person does an act without such an offer, he is not entitled to any reward.
- Since *ja'alah* is not binding on the offeree, it is not necessary for him to accept the offer, even if the reward is offered to a specific person. Acceptance by the doer is not a condition of the *ja'alah* contract.
- The Maliki is also stipulated that the offeror must be deriving a benefit from the task. Thus, they would not permit a person to pay a reward to anyone who climbs a mountain. The Shafi'is, on the other hand, did not stipulate that condition, but required that the task must involve some difficulty to warrant compensation.[8]

According to the Malikis Shafi'is and Hanbalis the offeror may withdraw his offer of reward prior to the commencement of the work by the offeree. However, once the offeree begins the work the contract is binding on the offeror, while the offeree may still withdraw from the contract. If an offeror withdraws his offer of reward after the offeree begins the work then the offeror is bound to pay the worker the going market wage for the work he had done.[9]

The differences between the contracts of *Ijarah* and *Ja'alah*:

- In *Ja'alah,* a worker/offeree is not paid in advance unless the action is completely done, whereas in *ijarah,* an employee could be paid for his work even if the job is not complete.
- In *Ja'alah,* the ambiguity (*gharar*) about the amount of service or its duration is tolerated on the ground that the contract is revocable. In *ijarah,* on the other hand, the amount of service and its duration should be known.
- *Ja'alah* is a nonbinding contract that can be revoked at any time, whereas *ijarah* is a binding contract.
- Unlike *Ijarah,* the person who performs the service may not be known.
- In an employment (*ijarah*), the employee must be paid in cash, whereas in a contract of reward (*ja'alah*), the doer could be paid in pecuniary or nonpecuniary means. For example, a doer could be paid in cash, given a car, a house, a title, a medal, or a promotion.

- It is possible to combine the reward in a *ja'alah* and salary in an employment (*ijarah*) contract. For instance, an employee could be offered a reward in addition to his salary if he performs additional tasks or meets certain other requirements.

The differences between the contracts of *Ja'alah* and *Hiba:*

- A gift is given to appreciate someone's past deeds or to strengthen relationships, whereas in *ja'alah,* the reward is offered for a service to be performed later.
- A gift is a gratuitous contract, whereas *ja'alah* is not.

Chapter Questions

True/False

1. ( ) In a lease contract, the right to use the leased asset and its ownership is transferred to the lessee.
2. ( ) The risk of deliberate destruction of the leased asset should be borne by the lessor.
3. ( ) The risk of depreciation of the leased asset should be borne by the lessor.
4. ( ) At the end of the operational lease, the leasing company transfers the ownership of the leased asset to the customer.
5. ( ) Usufruct refers to a tangible benefit such as the wage or salary of an employee.
6. ( ) A person should not be paid for the performance of a job that is his obligation to perform.
7. ( ) An employee should not be paid from the produce of his work.
8. ( ) In *i'arah,* the maintenance expenses of the borrowed item should be paid by the borrower.
9. ( ) A person may not rent his trees for their fruits.
10. ( ) The contract of reward (*ja'alah*) is not valid if the offer made is not accepted by the worker (*'amil*).
11. ( ) It is not valid to make an offer of reward (*ja'alah*) for a specific person.
12. ( ) It is valid to make an offer of reward (*ja'alah*) for unknown persons.

Short Answer

1. Should the government introduce a policy that would set a minimum wage to the employees or should the determination of wages be left to the market and contracting parties?
2. ABC Sdn Bhd, which owns several rubber plantations, has decided to pay its employees a specified amount of raw rubber as wages for their services. Discuss the validity of this decision.
3. Briefly discuss the responsibility of the lessor and the lessee with regard to the maintenance of leased asset.

4. State what the main differences are between the contracts of reward (*ji'alah*) and employment (*ijarah*)?
5. Explain why it is permitted for a person to lease his house but not his money.
6. Discuss the classification of employees into special employee (*ajir al-khas*) and common employee (*ajir al-'aam*).

Notes

1. Al-Hafiz Abi Abdullah ibn Yazid al-Qazwini, *Sunan Ibn Maja* (Dar al-Fikir, Beirut: 2003), 566.
2. See Wahbah al-Zuhaili, *Financial Transactions in Islamic Jurisprudence*, vol.1, trans. Mahmoud A. El-Gamal (Beirut: Dar al-Fikr al-Mouaser, 2003), 399–400.
3. *Al-Hafiz al-zayla'i*, vol. 4, 131. See also al-Zuhaili.
4. al-Zuhaili, p. 400.
5. Shariah Standard No. 9, Ijarah and Ijarah Muntahia Bittamleek, AAOIFI: Shariah Standards 1425–6H/2004–5, pp. 135–158, at p. 151.
6. For a discussion see al-Zuhaili, *Financial Transactions in Islamic Jurisprudence*, 609–610.
7. See Abu al-Walid Muhammad ibn Ahmad ibn Rushd, *Bidayat al-Mujtahid wa Nihayat al-Muqtasid*, vol. 2 (Beirut: Dar al-Kutub al-'Ilmiyyah, 2003), 360.
8. See al-Zuhaili, *Financial Transactions in Islamic Jurisprudence*, 440.
9. Ibid, 441.

CHAPTER

4

The Contract of Agency (*Wakalah*)

Learning outcomes

At the end of this chapter, you should be able to:

1. Identify the main constituent pillars and important conditions of the contract.
2. Explain the types of *wakalah* contract and their different uses.
3. Understand issues related to the agency in sale and agency in purchase.
4. Differentiate between agency and other types of legal relationships.

Introduction

Wakalah literally means protection, delegation, or authorisation. Legally, *wakalah* refers to a contract in which a person who has complete legal capacity authorises another to conclude a certain well-defined permissible contract on his behalf. An agent (*wakil*) establishes contractual relations between a principal (*asil/muwakkil*) and a third party.

The main purpose of an agency is to facilitate economic exchanges between a principal and third parties when such exchanges are hindered by distance, numbers, or when the principal is unable or unwilling to act personally. Agency is also necessitated by the fact that an agent has to perform certain tasks that the principal has neither the time, knowledge, nor expertise to perform him- or herself. For example, a real estate agent is appointed to sell or purchase a certain property on behalf of the principal. In some cases, distance may prevent a person from personally concluding a commercial transaction. The person may appoint an agent to enter into the contract on his or her behalf. Agency is also necessitated in some other cases by the presence of many customers in one or different locations. For instance, insurance or travel agents could be appointed to deal with many customers in various locations. In organisations such as companies, managers and directors are needed to act on behalf of the companies.

The main features of agency are representation, the provision of service, and power to affect the legal position of the principal. As shown in Figure 4.1, a principal authorises an agent to represent him. An agent, therefore, provides a service to the principal. Because an agent represents the principal, he can acquire rights for his principal and can subject him to liabilities. An agent is entitled to receive a commission for his services. If payment is not mentioned, then reference is made to the going market commission for that work. For example, an agent in sale,

FIGURE 4.1 In a *wakalah* contract, an agent represents a principal and acts on his behalf. The agent may receive a commission for providing the service.

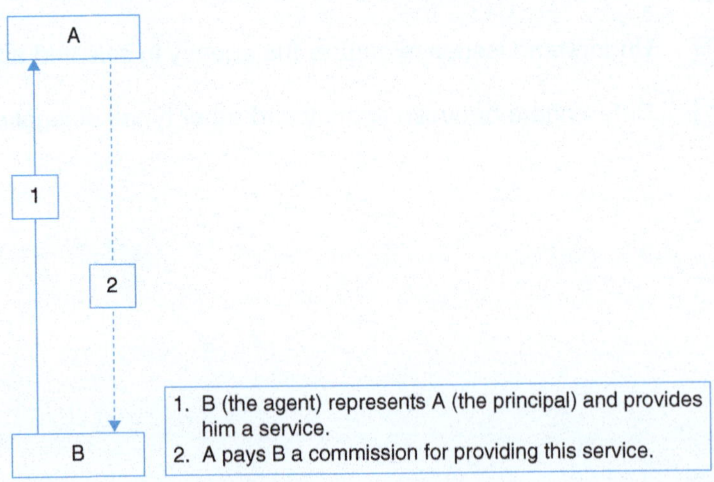

an agent in purchase, or a debt-collection agent is entitled to a commission in accordance with the going market rate common among the people.

An agent is in fiduciary relationship with the principal, which is based on trust, and, therefore, the agent should disclose all the information related to the property to the principal.

The Pillars of an Agency (*Wakalah*) Contract

According to the Hanafiis, an agency contract has two pillars of offer and acceptance. The majority of the jurists state that the contract of *wakalah* is based on four pillars. They are: the principal (*muwakkil*), agent (*wakil*), subject-matter of an agency, and by the parties, which includes offer and acceptance.

The conditions of an agency (*Wakalah*) contract include:

- The principal should have the required legal capacity to become a party to a contract. If a person, due to the lack of legal capacity, cannot conclude a contract himself, he cannot authorise an agent to conclude that contract on his behalf. For example, insane individuals or minors cannot appoint agents to act on their behalf. Instead they need guardians to act on their behalf.
- The agent should also have the requisite legal capacity. He must know of the agency contract and understand the nature of the contract he is concluding on behalf of the principal.
- The principal and the agent should know each other, and the act for which an agent is authorised to perform should be known. This is to avoid ambiguity (*gharar*).
- The act for which an agent is authorised to perform should be permissible. Agency is not allowed in usurpation or in taking others' property unlawfully.
- The act for which an agent is authorised must be eligible for legal representation. For instance, it is possible to appoint an agent to sell, purchase, or rent a certain property. It is also possible to appoint an agent to collect debts, to borrow or lend money, or to take or return deposits. In contrast, agency is not permissible in matters of worship like prayer and fasting. It is also not permissible to appoint an agent to give evidence or to take oath on behalf of the principal.[1] However, the majority of the jurists have permitted agency in acts of worship that have financial dimension. For instance, it is possible for a person to authorise another to pay or receive *zakat* or charities, to slaughter sacrificial animals, or to perform hajj on his behalf. According to the Hanafiis, it is also not permissible to appoint an agent to gain ownership over public or common properties. For example, a person cannot appoint an agent to collect wood or fruits from trees in a forest or to fish in a river for him because wood, fruits, and fish in these cases are considered common properties that belong to both the principal as well as the agent. In such cases the agent is deemed to be the owner of these properties as the rule of first possession is applicable here. However, the Malikis, Hanbalis, and most Shafi'i jurists argue for the permissibility of such an agency.[2]

The Types of Agency

An agent's authority is derived and defined by the particular type of agency he undertakes. Based on the authority of the agent, *wakalah* can be divided into the following types.

Particular Agency (al-Wakalah al-Khaassah)

In a particular agency, a principal authorises an agent to conclude a certain known transaction on his behalf. For example, a principal may appoint an agent to sell his car or to purchase a house for him. In this case, the agent is authorised to sell or buy only that particular house or car.

General Agency (al-Wakalah al-'Aammah)

A general agency is a type of agency in which a principal delegates full authority and power to an agent to act and perform a series of transactions on his behalf. For example, a principal may authorise an agent to purchase a house, lease it to others, collect its rental, and maintain the house in good condition. In this case, the agent owns all the power that the principal has with regard to the house. A director of a company could also be an example of a general agency because he has full power and authority to act and enter into a series of transactions on behalf of the company. A general agency is not restricted to a particular contract but may involve a series of contracts. The Hanafiis and Malikis have argued in favour of a general agency on the grounds that because agency is valid with regard to each individual transaction, it is also valid with regard to a series of transactions.

> *A director of a company could also be an example of a general agency because he has full power and authority to act and enter into a series of transactions on behalf of the company.*

Restricted Agency (al-Wakalah al-Mu'allaqa)

According to Hanafii and Hanbali jurists, agency could be either restricted or unrestricted. According to them, agency could be deferred or restricted by conditions. A restricted agent has to act within certain conditions. For example, a principal may instruct him to purchase a house at a particular time at the future or sell a property only to a particular person, to purchase a property from a known person, or to purchase a property for a cash price or based on instalments. The agent has to strictly observe these conditions. If the conditions are not observed, the agent concludes the transaction for himself and it is not binding on the principal.

Unrestricted Agency (al-Wakalah al-Mutlaqah)

An unrestricted agency is a type of agency in which an agent is not restricted by any conditions in the conclusion of a certain transaction—for example, when a principal authorises an agent to sell or purchase a house and the principal does not specify the time for its sale or purchase, the person to whom the house should be sold or from whom it should be purchased, or when a principal does not specify the method of price payment. However, an agent is still bound to act within the limits of common practices and customs (*'urftijari*). Imam Abu Hanifah argues that an agent is not bound by the customs because it differs from place to place. However, according to his two disciples and the majority of the jurists, the agent is bound to observe the custom common among the people. If he acts contrary to the custom, the execution of the transaction depends on the approval of the principal.

Agency in Sale

Agency in sale refers to an agency in which a principal appoints an agent to sell a certain property for him, as shown in Figure 4.2. If the principal restricts the authority of the agent by imposing certain conditions, the agent is bound to observe them. If the agent concludes a contract that contravenes the terms and conditions of the agency, the contract is not binding on the principal and its validity depends on his approval. For cases in which an agent concludes a contract that apparently contravenes the conditions, but the contract is beneficial to the principal, it is binding on the principal—for example, if A authorises B to sell his property at a certain price, but B sells the property at a higher price.

If an agent is given absolute authority according to Imam Abu Hanifah, he may act on his discretion. However, the majority of the jurists are of the view that an absolute agent is bound by the commercial customs common among the people. For example, he cannot pay for stamp duty and other expenses for the transfer of ownership if the commercial customs of the locality require the purchaser to pay for them. Similarly, he cannot sell the property for a price lower than the market price or in exchange for other commodities.[3]

An agent in sale is not allowed to buy the property himself, or to sell it to his wife, father, son, or other close relatives because this may involve clash of interest. When an agent who is authorised to sell a property to others himself purchases the property, the following conflict of interests and moral hazards may arise:

- A principal naturally wants to sell the property for a higher price. He wants to see more offers and prices, whereas an agent would like to purchase the property for a lower price. It may result in granting the agent a sort of monopoly power because he would be the sole purchaser.
- The agent may be tempted not to sell the property to a potential purchaser who bid a higher price. He may hide this fact from the principal. Because the agent wants to purchase the property, the agent may not try to obtain the best possible price.

FIGURE 4.2 A appointed B as his agent to sell a property. B sells the property to C. B receives the price from C and transfers it to A. A gives B a commission for his service.

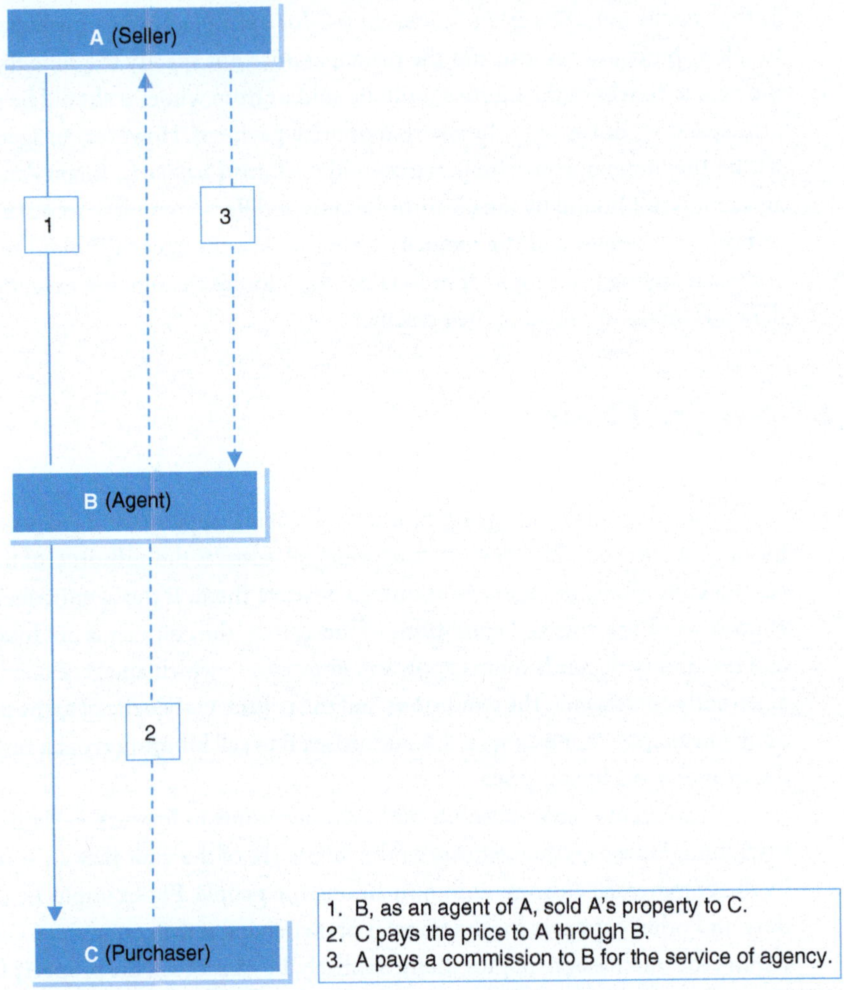

- An agent is usually an expert about market conditions and has vast experience in sale and purchase of properties. In contrast, a principal is only interested in selling his property. An agent knows more about the market than a principal. The agent may know that the market price will increase and the property could be sold for a higher price. The agent could be tempted to purchase the property and later sell it to others for a higher price.
- An agent may have insider knowledge and confidential information about the principal's financial status, such as the principal's need for a quick sale and the fact that the principal is willing to sell the property below the market price. There is a possibility that an agent may use this opportunity to advantage and to the detriment of his principal.

- An agent may hide information from a principal or give the principal incorrect information in order to purchase the principal's property.
- An agent is paid a commission for a service. The agent should not use this opportunity to make profit at the cost of the principal.

An agent should not take undue advantage of his or her position and become a purchaser at the same time. If an agent wants to purchase the property, he or she should withdraw from the agency contract. The principal may appoint a new agent who would decide to whom the property should be sold. If an agent purchases the property, the principal has the right to cancel the contract.

Agency in Purchase

Agency in purchase refers to a situation in which a principal authorises an agent to purchase a certain property, as shown in Figure 4.3. An agent in purchase may be restricted to certain conditions with regard to the price or description of the property, or the agent may be given full authority. If a restricted agent goes beyond his or her authority, the purchase is not binding on the principal, unless it is beneficial to the principal.

An agent in purchase is prohibited to purchase the property for him- or herself. If a principal authorises an agent to purchase a certain known property, such as a specified piece of land or a house, the agent should not purchase that property for him- or herself or for others. The agent may be tempted to purchase the property and resell it to the principal at a higher price. Similarly, an agent in purchase is not allowed to buy the property from him- or herself (to sell his or her own property to the principal) or to buy it from other close relatives. When an agent, who is authorised to purchase a property, sells his or her property to a principal, the following conflict of interests and moral hazards may arise:

- A principal naturally wants to purchase the property for a lower price, whereas an agent would like to sell it for a higher price.
- An agent may also hide the defect of the property he or she sells to the principal.
- An agent in purchase may not try to purchase the property for a lower price because he or she has his or her own interest to sell his or her property to the principal.
- An agent may also be tempted to sell his or her property to a principal knowing well that the value of the property will go down.
- An agent may also be tempted to hide information from a principal or give the principal incorrect information in order to sell his or her property to the principal.
- An agent is paid commission for his or her service. He or she should not use this opportunity to make profit by selling his or her property to a principal.

If an agent wants to sell his or her property to a principal, he or she should first withdraw from the agency contract. The principal may appoint a new agent who would decide from whom the property should be purchased. If an agent sells his or her property to a principal, the principal has the right to cancel the sale contract.

FIGURE 4.3 A appointed B as his agent to purchase a property. B purchases the property from C. B receives the price from A and transfers it to C. A gives B commission for his service.

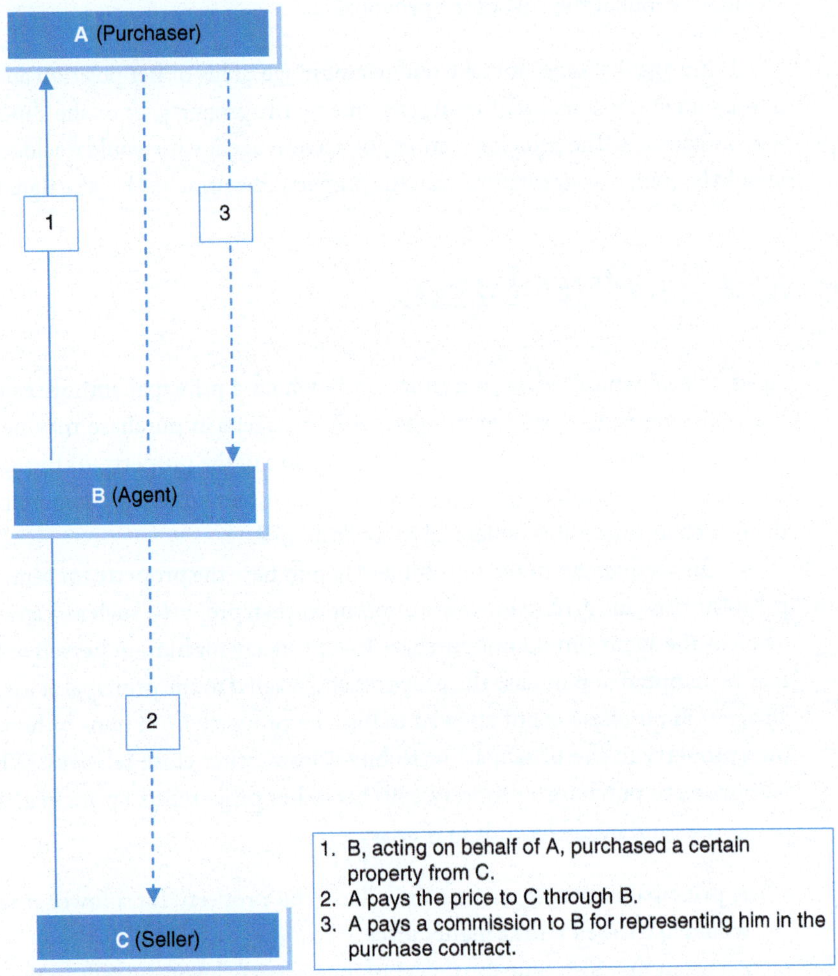

The Effects and the Rights and Liabilities of the Contracting Parties

The scholars agree that all legal effects (*hukm*) that result from a contract concluded by an agent go directly to the principal. For instance, the ownership of a certain property bought by an agent is automatically transferred to the principal. However, there are differences of opinion on whether the ensuing rights and liabilities that may result from a certain contract should be enforced by the principal himself or through the agent. These may include, for instance, taking possession of the sold item, collecting the price, and exercising the option of defect and other options in a sale contract. The Hanbalis are of the opinion that because an agent derives his authority from the principal and acts on the principal's behalf, the ensuing rights and liabilities should also be attributed to the principal who may perform them. They argue that an agent is only representing the principal party and facilitates the conclusion of a contract. Once the contract is concluded, the agent withdraws and all the legal effects, rights, and liabilities should be attributed to the principal. The Hanafi, Shafi'i, and Maliki *Fiqh* schools, however, are of the opinion that, if a contract is a type of contract in which an agent should directly attribute to the principal, then the ensuing rights and liabilities of the contract should be exercised by the principal. These include contracts in which the physical presence and the actual transfer of the subject matter are necessary (*'uqud al-'ainiyyah*), such as the contracts of gift, borrowing (*i'arah*), loan (*qard*), deposit (*wadi'ah*), and pledge. The agent, when concluding these contracts, should specifically attribute these contracts to the principal and mention the principal's name. For instance, the agent should say that he or she has given a gift from the property of the principal, or he has deposited the property of the principal, or he has borrowed for the principal. Subsequently, the ensuing rights and liabilities of these contracts should be attributed to the principal and could be enforced by and against him. The principal in these contracts should deliver the gift to the receiver and claim the deposit, and the creditor can directly claim the settlement of debt from him. If an agent, while concluding these contracts, does not attribute them to the principal, then he concludes these contracts for him- or herself and not for the principal. They further argue that, in all other contracts, regardless of whether an agent directly attributes them to the principal, the agent should exercise the ensuing rights and liabilities. For instance, an agent is solely liable to deliver the sold item, collect the price, and exercise the option of defect and other options. The principal cannot ask for the possession of the sold item. The principal also cannot demand the price from the purchaser or exercise the options. The principal has to exercise these rights through the agent. These schools are of the opinion that the purpose of the agency is to relieve the principal from doing acts for which he or she personally has no ability or time. If the principal is to perform these acts, the principal may not benefit from the contract of agency.[4]

An Agent Appointing Another Agent

There is an agreement among jurists that, in a restricted agency, an agent is not allowed to appoint another agent. Exceptions are made for cases in which the commissioned task could not be accomplished by a single agent and requires the help of other agents or for cases in which the task requires the contribution of other skills. In such cases, an agent may appoint another agent with the permission of the principal. Then, both would become the agents for the same principal. In an unrestricted agency, an agent may appoint another agent, and the new agent is considered as an agent of the principal together with the first agent.

In an unrestricted agency, an agent may appoint another agent, and the new agent is considered as an agent of the principal together with the first agent.

Unauthorised Agency (*al-Fadhalah*)

Fadhuli literally means the involvement of a person in activities that do not concern that person. Legally, it refers to a contract made by a person on behalf of another person without any authorisation. It happens, for instance, if an unauthorised person purchases a certain property for another.

The Shafiis, Hanbalis, and the Zahiris are of the opinion that the contract or actions of a *fadhuli* are void, even if it is ratified later. They argue that a subsequent ratification cannot validate a void contract. According to them, a contract concluded by a *fadhuli* is void *ab initio* because he or she is neither an owner of the property nor a guardian or an agent who is authorised to act on behalf of another. Consequently, there is no valid contract to be approved. The Hanafis and the Malikis, on the other hand, view the contract of a *fudhuli* as validly concluded. However, the contract can only be executed and produce its legal effects when it is approved by the person on whose behalf it is made.

Termination of an Agency

The Maliki and Hanafii jurists argue that an agency contract (*wakalah*) in which an agent is paid commission is binding, whereas the Shafi'i and Hanbali jurists argue that agency is a nonbinding contract.[5] An agency (*wakalah*) contract may come to an end in the following cases:

- When a principal terminates the agency contract. The termination is valid provided the agent is informed and such a termination does not affect the third party's right.
- When a principal him- or herself performs the transaction for which he or she has appointed an agent.
- When the reason for which an agency is made no longer exists.
- When either a principal or his or her agent is disqualified or lose their legal capacity—for example, when one of them becomes bankrupt.
- When the object for which an agency is made has perished.
- When an agent withdraws from the agency contract. The agent should inform the principal of his or her withdrawal.

The Differences Between the Contracts of Wakalah *and Employment (*Ijarah*)*

An employee is a person who is completely subject to the control of his employer about what he does and how he does it. For instance, a servant in a shop sells a thing as an assistant of the owner, and he does not represent his employer. An agent, on the other hand, is given authority to perform a certain transaction on behalf of a principal. The following are the main differences between the contracts of agency and employment:

- An agent is representing a principal and establishes contractual relationship between the principal and a third party, whereas an employee is not a representative of the employer.
- An agent receives his commission upon performance of the job, whereas an employee is entitled to his salary regardless of whether the job is done.
- An agent may receive more commission when more goods are sold, whereas an employee receives his fixed salary.
- An agent has no fixed time to perform a job, which may take longer or shorter time. An employee, on the other hand, has to finish the job within a specified time. In other words duration is not taken into account when an agent is paid his commission, whereas in an employment contract, duration is the basis for the payment.
- An agent can work for more than one principal at a time, whereas a full-time employee cannot work for another employer.
- An agent may, in certain circumstances, appoint another agent, whereas an employee cannot appoint another employee.
- An employee is entitled to employment benefits such as health benefits, holidays, bonuses, and so forth, whereas an agent is not.
- Agency is not a binding contract. An agent, except in certain circumstances, can be dismissed at any time. Employment (*Ijarah*) is a binding contract. An employee must always be given notice or must be dismissed for some lawful justification.
- An agent can choose his or her own way of doing work and decide when he or she should do it or how he or she should do it. An employee, on the other hand, has to work for the employer under the employer's instructions and control.

The Differences Between the Contracts of Wakalah *and Reward (*Ja'alah*)*

The following is the difference between the contracts of *wakalah* and *ja'alah*:

- In *ja'alah*, a worker/offeree does a simple task, such as finding a lost property, designing the best logo, or discovering a certain cure for a disease. In contrast, in an agency (*wakalah*) contract, an agent enters into a certain contractual relationship with a third party on behalf of the principal.

Chapter Questions

True/False

1. ( ) According to the majority of the *Fiqh* schools, a seller who sells a certain item through an agent for a deferred price should also claim the price through the agent.
2. ( ) According to the majority of the *Fiqh* schools, an absolute agent is bound to act in accordance with the prevailing commercial practices of a society.

3. ( ) All scholars agree that the ownership of a certain property bought by an agent is automatically transferred to the principal.
4. ( ) An agent in purchase is not allowed to sell his own property to the principal.
5. ( ) An agent in sale may buy the property of the principal for the same price that others are willing to pay.
6. ( ) If an agent appoints another agent, both the original agent and the new agent are considered agents for the same principal.
7. ( ) Because a minor cannot enter into a transaction, he may appoint an agent to conclude the transaction on his behalf.
8. ( ) The Hanafii jurists argue that an absolute or unrestricted agent is still bound by the common and current commercial practices of a community.
9. ( ) The schools of *Fiqh* differ on whether a purchaser who has purchased a certain item through an agent should exercise the option of defect directly or through an agent.
10. ( ) When an absolute agent appoints another agent, the new agent is considered as an agent of the absolute agent.

Short Answer

1. Explain how conflict of interests may arise if an agent in sale or an agent in purchase sells the property to him- or herself or purchases it.
2. Briefly discuss why an agent who is appointed to purchase a certain property should not purchase that property for himself.
3. Briefly discuss why an agent who is appointed to sell a certain property should not purchase that property.
4. In your view, what are the factors that may necessitate agency?
5. State the differences between the contracts of employment (*ijarah*) and agency (*wakalah*).

Notes

1. See Wahbah al-Zuhaili, *Financial Transactions in Islamic Jurisprudence*, vol. 2, trans. Mahmoud A. El-Gamal (Beirut: Dar al-Fikr al-Mouaser, 2003), 640–641.
2. Ibid, 649.
3. See as-Sayyid Sabiq, *Fiqhu as-Sunnah* (Cairo: Dar al-Hadith, 2004), 970.
4. See Ramadhan Ali al-Sharanbasi, *Al-Nazariyat al-'Aamah fi al-Fiqh al-Islami* (al-Iskandariyyah: Munshaat al-M'arif, 2000), 108–109; Wahbah Zuhaili, *al-Fiqh al-Islami Wa Adillatuhu* (Damascus: Dar al-Fikir, 1989), 114–117.
5. For a discussion, see Wahbah al-Zuhaili, *Financial Transactions in Islamic Jurisprudence*, vol. 2, trans. Mahmoud A. El-Gamal (Beirut: Dar al-Fikr al-Mouaser, 2003), 683–689.

CHAPTER

5

The Contract of Loan (*al-Qard*)

Learning outcomes

At the end of this chapter, you should be able to:

1. Understand *qard* contract and its gratuitous and charitable nature.
2. Identify the main constituent pillars and important conditions of the contract.
3. Explain the differences between *qard*, *dayn*, and *i'arah.*
4. Understand the debate on the prohibition of conditional benefits that a lender may stipulate in a *qard* contract.

Introduction

Literally, *qard* means cutting off. It is called *qard* because, through this contract, a certain part of the lender's property is cut off and given to a borrower. *Qard,* as shown in Figure 5.1, refers to a gratuitous contract in which a lender gives a certain homogeneous (*mithli*) property to a borrower on the condition that the latter is responsible to return a similar property to the lender immediately upon demand.[1] Its effect is to unconditionally transfer the ownership of the loaned property to the borrower.

Islam has prohibited usury (*riba*) and allowed loan (*qard*). *Qard* refers to an interest-free loan intended to help a person who is in need of cash. The provision of cash to a person in need is a praiseworthy and recommended (*mandub*) act for which a Muslim is rewarded by Allah (swt). The gratuitous nature of the loan contract is established by *ahadith,* which have promised rewards to the lender. It is reported that the Prophet (pbAbuh) said, "In the night of the journey, I saw on the gate of heaven written, 'reward for *sadaqah* is ten times and reward for *qard* is eighteen times.' So, I asked the angel, how is it possible? The angel replied: 'Because a beggar who asked had already had something but a borrower did not ask for loan unless he was in need'. "[2]

أسري بي مكتوبا على باب الجنة الصدقة بعشر أمثالها والقرض بثمانية عشر فقلت يا جبريل ما للقرض أفضل من الصدقة قال لأن الانسان يسأل وعنده الشيء والمستقرض لا يستقرض إلا من حاجة رأيت ليلة

In another *Hadith* reported by Abu Hurairah (mAbpwh), the Prophet (pbAbuh) said, "Whoever relieves a believer from a difficulty in this world, Allah will relieve him from his difficulty and Allah (swt) will facilitate him in this world and world hereafter."[3]

من نفس عن أخيه كربة من كرب الدنيا ، نفس الله بها عنه كربة من كرب يوم القيامة

FIGURE 5.1 B borrows a certain amount of money from A and undertakes to return the same amount to A at a future date.

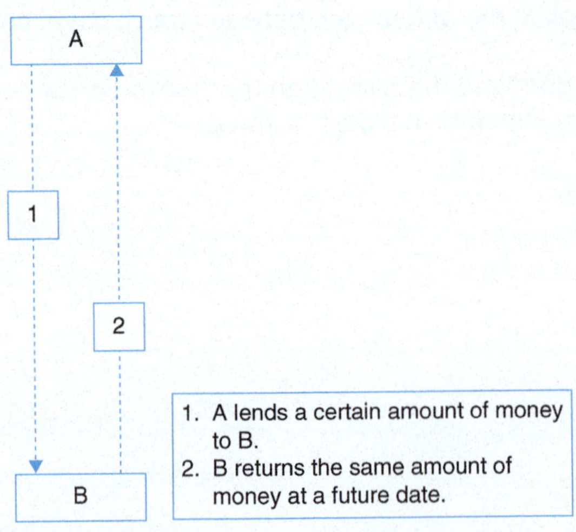

Loan (*Qard*), Debt (*Dayn*), and Borrowing Things (*I'arah*)

Another similar but wider concept is *dyan,* which is not necessarily gratuitous. Although *qard* is created by the provision of cash to a borrower, a *dayn* comes into existence when the settlement of a certain financial right created through contracts is postponed to future—for instance, deferred or unpaid price in a sale contract or deferred or unpaid rental in a lease contract, unpaid dower, or unpaid damages are considered *dayn. Dayn* can also arise when a person lends his money to another, whereas *qard* is more specific and may arise only through a loan contract. Thus, debt (*dayn*) is a broader concept than loan (*qard*). Hence every *qard* is a *dayn,* but not vice versa.[4]

I'arah is a contract in which an owner gives a certain usable property to a borrower without consideration. The borrower of the property temporarily and gratuitously owns the usufruct. This contract is encouraged and recommended as a form of permissible and charitable deed. The property is held on trust by the borrower, who is therefore not liable for its destruction, loss, or diminution of value, unless caused intentionally or by his fault and negligence. In *i'arah,* the ownership of the borrowed item is not transferred to the borrower. He has to return the same item at a stipulated time. However, in lending (*qard*), the ownership of the borrowed money is transferred to the borrower. The borrower doesn't have to return the same money/notes; it can be any other notes.

Important conditions for a loan (*qard*) contract include:

- Both the lender and the borrower should have complete legal capacity to enter into a *qard* contract.
- The loaned money should be transferred to the borrower and should come to his possession. There is no loan contract if the borrower does not take possession of the money.
- The borrower should acquire an absolute and unconditional ownership right to use and appropriate the borrowed money.
- The borrowed and repaid money must be equal and belong to the same currency. The borrower is under obligation to return an equal amount of the same currency. The condition concerning the spontaneous exchange of *ribawi* properties is not applicable to *qard* contract. This exception is made to enable the person in need to borrow money and to return it later. For instance, a person who borrows money in Ringgit Malaysia must return it in the same currency.
- According to the majority of the *Fiqh* schools there should not be any specific date for the settlement of a loan (*qard*). Specifying a date for the settlement of a loan, according to them, would change the charitable nature of the contract. Thus, a borrower may return the loan at any time when he has the ability to do so. A lender may also demand the settlement of the loan at any time when he needs the money. However, it is recommended that a lender should give more time to a borrower who, due to financial constraints, could not settle the loan. The Malikis, on the other hand, argue that a lender and a borrower may agree on a specific date for the settlement of the loan. The majority of jurists have differentiated between *dayn* and

qard. They define *dayn* as an obligation to be settled in a certain known period, whereas *qard* is an obligation that could be settled at any time. This, they argue, is due to the gratuitous nature of the *qard* contract. The Malikis, however, do not distinguish between *qard* and *dayn*. They argue that Muslims are free to put any condition in a transaction except a condition that makes a permissible act/thing forbidden or forbids a permissible act/thing. According to Malikis, when the time for the settlement of a loan is specified, the lender is not allowed to request the borrower to return the loan prior to the fixed specified time.

- The loan should be settled in lump sum upon demand by the lender.
- A lender should not stipulate that the borrower should settle the loan at another place.
- There should not be any condition that would entitle the lender to any return or benefit.

*In lending (*qard*), the ownership of the borrowed money is transferred to the borrower. In* i'arah*, the ownership of the borrowed item is not transferred to the borrower.*

A Loan That Provides Conditional Benefit to the Lender

Any stipulation in a *qard* contract that benefits the lender is prohibited. The *qard* contract must be free of any expected return or benefit to the lender. Any stipulated return or benefit to the lender amounts to *riba* and is prohibited. The principle regarding stipulated benefit to the lender is derived from the *Hadith,* which states, "any loan which results in a benefit is considered a form of usury."[5]

كل قرض جر منفعة فهو وجه من وجوه الربا

Muslim jurists from different *Fiqh* schools, while discussing the *Hadith,* deduced the general principle that any benefit gained from the loan by the lender is considered usury if the benefit is stipulated in the loan agreement.[6] All jurists agree that any condition that a debtor should return any additional amount over and above the loan is prohibited, whether the additional property belongs to the same type as the loan property or comes from a different type. It also does not matter whether the additional amount is excessive or little. A lender is prohibited from stipulating any condition that would provide him with a benefit because it amounts to usury. It also negates the gratuitous nature of the loan contract.[7] Qurtubi says, "there is a consensus among Muslim jurists based on the tradition from the Prophet (pbAbuh) that any stipulation for increase in a loan contract is usury even though it is a fistful of forage as mentioned by Ibn Mas'ud or a single grain.[8] However, if a borrower voluntarily returns the borrowed money in higher quality, quantity, or value, such an act is commendable. Similarly, if a lender is willing to take back the loaned money in lesser or lower quality, quantity, or value, of his free will, this act is also regarded as commendable.

However, there are some exceptions to this legal rule. A lender may accept noncontractual or noncustomary unstipulated benefit from the borrower. A borrower may voluntarily return the loan with an additional amount or in a better quality. This is not only allowed but is recommended. Abu Hurariah (mAbpwh) narrated that the Prophet (pbAbuh) is reported to have said, "The best amongst you is the one who pays the rights of others generously."[9]

إن خياركم أحسنكم قضاء

There are also other narrations that support the legality of unstipulated benefit to the lender. Abu Rafi' reported that Allah's Messenger (pbAbuh) took from a man as a loan a young camel (less than six years). Then the camels of Sadaqa were brought to him. He ordered Abu Rafi' to return to that person the young camel (as a return of the loan). Abu Rafi' returned to him and said, "I did not find among them but better camels above the age of six." He (the Prophet) said, "Give that to him for the best men are those who are best in paying off the debt."[10]

رسول الله صلى الله عليه وسلم استسلف من رجل بَكْراً، فقدمت عليه إبل من إبل الصدقة، فأمر أبا رافع أن يقضي الرجل بَكْرَه،
فرجع إليه أبو رافع فقال: لم أجد فيها إلا خياراً رباعياً. فقال: أعطه إياه، إن خيار الناس أحسنهم قضاءً أن

Jabir bin Abdullah (mAbpwh) is reported to have said that the Prophet (pbAbuh) "paid me the debt he owed me and gave me an extra amount."[11]

وَكَانَ لِي عَلَيْهِ دَيْنٌ فَقَضَانِي وَزَادَنِي

In another narration by Abu Huraira it is reported: "A man demanded his debts from Allah's Apostle in such a rude manner that the companions of the Prophet intended to harm him, but the Prophet said, 'Leave him, no doubt, for he (the creditor) has the right to demand it (harshly). Buy a camel and give it to him.' They said, 'The camel that is available is older than the camel he demands.' The Prophet said, 'Buy it and give it to him, for the best among you are those who repay their debts handsomely'."[12]

هريرة رضي الله عنه أَنَّ رَجُلًا تَقَاضَى رَسُولَ اللَّهِ صَلَّى اللَّهُ عَلَيْهِ وَسَلَّمَ فَأَغْلَظَ لَهُ فَهَمَّ بِهِ أَصْحَابُهُ فَقَالَ دَعُوهُ فَإِنَّ لِصَاحِبِ الْحَقِّ
مَقَالًا وَاشْتَرُوا لَهُ بَعِيرًا فَأَعْطُوهُ إِيَّاهُ وَقَالُوا لَا نَجِدُ إِلَّا أَفْضَلَ مِنْ سِنِّهِ قَالَ اشْتَرُوهُ فَأَعْطُوهُ إِيَّاهُ فَإِنَّ خَيْرَكُمْ أَحْسَنُكُمْ قَضَاعن أبى

Based on these *Ahadith*, there is a consensus among the jurists on the permissibility of unstipulated benefits to the lender. This is in line with the benevolence that the Prophet (pbAbuh) encouraged strongly.

However, it is prohibited for a lender to receive gifts from a frequent borrower[13] or where there is a custom allowing the lender to receive some type of benefit from the loan, or where there exists a prior agreement allowing the lender to benefit from the loan.[14]

Waiting or Giving Time to a Borrower Is a Commendable Act

If a person is defaulting in payment due to financial constraints, then the person must be given respite until he or she is in a position to pay. However, it is more virtuous to forgive the person altogether. Allah (swt) states: "If the debtor is in a difficulty, grant him time till it is easy for him to repay. But if ye remit it by way of charity, that is best for you, if ye only knew" (2:280). A debtor who is defaulting without any valid excuse cannot be charged an extra amount as a penalty because this will constitute *riba*. Similarly, charging interest with the intention of giving it for charity is not permissible. Interest is unlawful, whether used for personal needs or given in charity. On the other hand, a debtor who is able to settle the debt should not delay to pay back his or her obligations. As the Prophet (pbAbuh) said: "Procrastination (delay) in repaying debts by a wealthy person is injustice."[15]

قَالَ رَسُولُ اللَّهِ صَلَّى اللَّهُ عَلَيْهِ وَسَلَّمَ مَطْلُ الْغَنِيِّ ظُلْمٌ

When a borrower dies, all his or her debts that are payable at a certain future fixed date are dissolved and become current loans. The *Qur'an* commands (4:12) that the debts of the deceased debtor must be paid before any distribution of the estate should take place. The heirs of the deceased are responsible to pay his/her debts from his/her property. All debts should be repaid immediately. The Prophet (pbuh) would not pray funeral prayer (*janazah*) on those dead persons who were in debt until the debt was settled. Similarly, bankruptcy will also dissolve debts payable at a certain fixed future time. It is possible in a *qard* contract that a creditor may demand that a guarantor guarantee the settlement of the loan or may insist on a pledge as a collateral security. If a borrower fails to pay back the loan, the creditor may ask the guarantor to pay or the borrower may sell the collateral security for the repayment of the loan.

If a person is defaulting in payment due to financial constraints, then the person must be given respite until he or she is in a position to pay.

Chapter Questions

True/False

1. ( ) A loan (*qard*) contract is concluded by the agreement of the parties even if the borrower does not take possession of the loaned money.

2. ( ) A lender in a loan (*qard*) contract can impose certain conditions about how the loaned money should be used.
3. ( ) According to the majority of the *Fiqh* schools, a lender can fix a certain date for the settlement of the loan.
4. ( ) If a loan is given for investment purposes, it is permissible for the lender to charge an additional amount for the use of his money.
5. ( ) Lending a computer or a book is an example of a *qard* contract.
6. ( ) Debts payable at a certain fixed future date should be paid immediately upon the debtor's death.
7. ( ) The borrower in a loan contract should acquire an absolute and unconditional right to use the money obtained by loan.
8. ( ) In a contract of loan (*qard*), the ownership of borrowed money is transferred to the borrower.
9. ( ) In a contract of loan (*qard*), it is permissible for a lender to stipulate that the loan should be settled in a different place or country.
10. ( ) It is permissible if a borrower voluntarily returns an additional amount over and above the principal to the lender.

Short Answer

1. Discuss the suitability of the interest-free loan (*qard*) contract for financing trade and businesses.
2. An important issue in a contract of loan is the depreciation of money due to inflation. If a person borrowed RM 10,000 and later wants to return the loan, should the person return the exact number, that is, RM 10,000, or should the person return the exact value that he has borrowed. The exact value of the loaned money at the settlement date may not necessarily correspond to the same figure of RM 10,000. Should the initial purchasing power of the money be taken into account when settling the loan?
3. Discuss the meaning of the principle that states that all loans that provide a conditional benefit to the lender are usurious.
4. A few years ago Ahmad lent Zaki $1000 when the exchange rate was RM 2.50 to one dollar and the amount lent was equal to RM 2,500. Because this was a *qard* contract, Ahmad agreed that Zaki would only pay back the loan when his financial status improved. Zaki now wants to settle the loan in Malaysian Ringgit 2500, based on the old exchange rate. Ahmad refuses to take the money and insists that Zaki should either pay $1000 or RM 3,000 based on the current exchange rate. Zaki argues that any additional amount beyond RM 2500 would be usury. Should the borrower pay in the same currency or in a different currency? If the borrower wants to pay in a different currency, should he pay based on the current exchange rate or should he pay based on the exchange rate of the day he borrowed the money? Discuss and advise the parties.

Notes

1. Al-Bahuti, Musa bin Younus, *Kashaf Al-Qina'*, vol. 3 (Beirut: Dar Al-Fikr, 1402), 312.
2. Ibn Majah, *Sunanibn Majah,* vol. 7, Hadith no. 2422, 276.
3. Abdul Hamid Siddiqui, *Translation of Sahih Muslim,* Book 35, no. 6505.
4. Hashiyaibn A'bideen: 169/4.
5. Imam al-Bayhaqi, *Sunan Al-Bayhaqi* (Makkah al-Mukarramah: Maktabah dar al-baz, 1994), vol. 5, p. 350, the book of sales 21, chapter of any loan which results in a benefit is considered usury 99, hadith no. 10705.
6. For a discussion, see Muhammad bin Ahmad Al-Sherbini, *Mughni Al-Muhtaj* (n.p.), vol. 2, 119.
7. Ibid.
8. Al-Qurtubi, *Al-Jami' li Ahkam Al-Qur'an,* vol. 3, 241.
9. Al-Qurtubi, Abu 'Abdullah. 1967. *Al-jami' li Ahkam al-Qur'an,* vol. 3, 241.
10. Muslim ibn Hajjaj, *Sahih,* Chapter: Man Istislafa sha'yan fa qada' khayran minhu, vol. 5, p. 54, Hadith no. 4192.
11. Al-Bukhari', *Sahih,* vol. 2, p. 786, Kitab al-Istiqrad 48, Bab Husn al-Qadha' 7, Hadith no. 2264; Muslim, *Sahih,* vol. 1, p. 495, Kitab al-Salah, Bab 'Istihbab Tahiyat al-Masjid', Hadith no. 715.
12. Al-Bukhari, *Sahih,* vol. 2, p. 785, Kitab al-Istqradh 48, Bab Istiqradh al-Ibil 4, Hadith no. 2260; Muslim, *Sahih,* vol. 3, p. 1225, Kitab al-Musaqah, Bab 'man Istaslaf Shaya'n Faqda Khayran minhu wa Khayrukum Ahsnukm Qada'n', Hadith no. 1601.
13. Sherbini, *Mughni al-Muhtaj,* vol. 2, p. 119. Hashiyat Ibn 'Abidin: vol. 4, pp. 174–296. Hashiyat al-Dasuqi: vol. 3, pp. 225–226. Ibn Qudamah, Al-Mughni, vol. 4, pp. 391–392.
14. Ibn 'Abidin, Muhammed 'Amin. 1987. *Hashiyat (Rad al-Mukhtarala ala-Dur al-Mukhtar),* vol. 4, 175; Al-Dasuqi, Muhammad ibn Ahmad. 1900. *Hashiyah,* vol. 3, 224; Al-Nawawi, Abu Zakaria. 1992. *Rawdhat al-Talibin,* vol. 2 (Beirut: Dar al-Kutub Al-Ilmiyyah), 279; Ibn Qudamah, *Al-Mughni,* vol. 4, 391.
15. *Sahih al-Bukhari,* trans. M. Muhsin Khan, vol. 3, book 41, no. 585.

CHAPTER 6

The Contract of Safekeeping (*al-Wadi'ah*)

Learning outcomes

At the end of this chapter, you should be able to:

1. Explain the main pillars and conditions of a *wadi'ah* contract.
2. Understand the nature of relationship between a depositor and a depository and circumstances in which a depository is held liable for any damage to the deposited property.
3. Understand the application of the *wadi'ah* contract by Islamic banks.
4. Compare and contrast deposit and loan contracts and to see the differences between gift (*hibah*) and interest.

Introduction

Literally, *wadi'ah* means deposit. Legally, it is a contract whereby a depositor leaves his property with another for the purpose of safekeeping. As shown in Figure 6.1, through *wadi'ah,* a person empowers another to keep and protect his property. The contract of *wadi'ah* is initiated by the owner of the deposit who needs to leave his property to the trust and care of a depository. Deposit (*wadi'ah*) refers to both the property and to the contract itself. The *Qur'an* in verse 4:58 commands: "Behold, God bids you to deliver all that you have been entrusted with unto those who are entitled thereto, and whenever you judge between people, to judge with justice. Verily, most excellent is what God exhorts you to do: verily, God is all-hearing, all-seeing!"

يَأْمُرُكُمْ أَن تُؤَدُّوا الْأَمَانَاتِ إِلَىٰ أَهْلِهَا وَإِذَا حَكَمْتُم بَيْنَ النَّاسِ أَن تَحْكُمُوا بِالْعَدْلِ ۚ إِنَّ اللَّـهَ نِعِمَّا يَعِظُكُم بِهِ ۗ إِنَّ اللَّـهَ كَانَ سَمِيعًا
بَصِيرًا إِنَّ اللَّـهَ

According to Imam Razi, "the term *amaanah* in this verse denotes anything one has been entrusted with, be it in the physical or moral sense."[1] During the pre-Islamic period, people in Mekkah would deposit their properties with the Prophet (pbAbuh) because of his well-known honesty and trustworthiness. Prior to his migration to Medina, the Prophet ordered Ali Ibn

FIGURE 6.1 In a *wadi'ah* contract, a person deposits his property with another for safekeeping purposes. The depository will return the deposit upon demand.

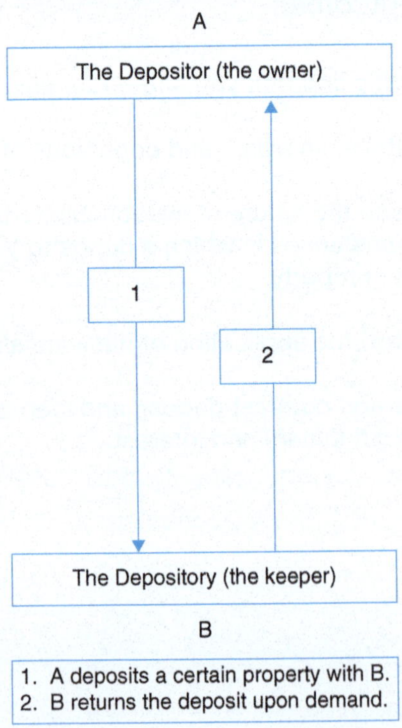

Abi Talib (mAbpwh) to stay behind in Mekkah in order to return the goods that people had deposited with him. This suggests that the practice of leaving one's property with others for the purpose of safekeeping (*wadi'ah*) was common among the Arabs before the advent of Islam and that the practice was endorsed by the Prophet (pbAbuh).

There is an agreement among all jurists that *wadi'ah* is a gratuitous and recommended (*mandub*) contract for which a depository could be rewarded by Allah (swt) for helping to keep a depositor's property. A depository, therefore, may not charge the depositor for safekeeping the deposit. However, a depository may charge the depositor if the deposited property needs special protection or involves expenses related to the accommodation and safekeeping of the deposit. For instance, a deposited property may occupy a large space, which may necessitate payment of rent or require special boxes or containers and protection that incur cost. A depository may also demand wages when safekeeping deposited properties become a fulltime job.

The contract of wadi'ah *is initiated by the owner of the deposit who needs to leave his property to the trust and care of a depository.*

The Pillars of *Wadi'ah* Contracts

According to the Hanafii jurists, the contract of *wadi'ah* has two pillars of offer and acceptance. The majority of jurists state that *wadi'ah* has four pillars. These include the depositor, the depository, the deposited property, and the expression of agreement that consists of offer (*ijaab*) and acceptance (*qabul*). Offer and acceptance can be both verbal or by indication. The Shafi'i jurists ruled that it is not necessary for the depository to accept the deposit verbally. According to them, the physical receipt of the deposited property by the depository amounts to the acceptance of the deposit.[2]

Important conditions of the *wadi'ah*:

- The parties should have complete legal capacity and should not suffer from obstacles to capacity such as minority, insanity, or bankruptcy.
- The depositary should keep a deposit in the same manner he keeps his own property.
- The property should be capable of being deposited. For instance, fruits and vegetables that could not be kept for a long time cannot be deposited.
- Any benefit that could be produced from the deposit belongs to the owner. For instance, when an animal is given for safekeeping, its young, milk, and wool belong to the owner.[3]
- The depository should also observe any other suitable conditions put by the depositor.

Relationship Between the Parties

The *hadith* of the Prophet (pbAbuh) has stated that a depository is not a guarantor. Based on this, the jurists agree that the status of a depository is that of a trustee. The principle that could be derived here is that a trustee cannot, at the same time, be considered a guarantor and that a trust and guarantee cannot be combined in one contract. As a trustee, his duty is to guard the interests of the depositor on whose behalf he holds the property. The depository is under an obligation to protect the deposited property in the same way as he protects his own property. He must take the necessary care expected from him as a trustee (*ameen*) with regard to the deposited property. He has to exert the same care as he would exert for safekeeping and protection of his own property and to render back the deposit when required. Accordingly, a depository is not obliged to guarantee the safety of the deposit or to compensate its losses. However, a depository is liable if there is evidence of negligence or usurpation on his part. If the deposited object is damaged, not due to any transgression or negligence on the part of the depository, he is not liable to replace it. He is considered to have taken all the necessary care as a trustee while keeping the deposited property. However, if the damage is caused due to the negligence or transgression on the part of the depository, he is liable to replace the object or to pay compensation.

When Is the Depository Held Liable?

In certain situations the status of a depository as a trustee could be changed to a guarantor where he is held liable for compensation and damages in case of any loss or damage to the deposit. These situations are:

- Intentional failure and neglect on the part of a depository that would expose the deposit to theft, fire, and other destructive causes.
- When a depository re-deposits the deposited property with another person without the depositor's permission.[4]
- A depository is held liable if the deposit is destroyed while he utilises it without the permission of the depositor.
- If a depository diverts the deposited money into his business in which he suffers losses, he is liable for the loss of the deposit. He is liable for any loss since he has diverted the sum of money which was deposited with him as a trust (*amanah*) to his own business.[5]
- A depository is held liable if he mixes the deposited property with his properties or other properties without the permission of the depositor and where separation of the properties is not possible.[6]
- A depository is held liable if he does not return the deposit to the depositor upon demand and the deposit is destroyed, damaged, or stolen. Refusals of the depository to return the deposit, and his denial that a deposit exists, are acts that amount to usurpation and entail liability.[7]
- A depository is held liable if he returns the deposit to someone else other than the depositor. If two persons jointly deposited a certain property with a depository and later one of them comes and asks that his share be returned to him, the preferred opinion is that it should be done with the permission of the other depositor. It is because the depository has no right to divide the deposited property.

- A depository should observe the instructions and conditions of the depositor concerning the method of safekeeping the deposited property. If a depository differs from those conditions and instructions and as a result of which the deposited property is damaged, he is held liable.
- A depository should not travel with the deposit. He should return the deposit to its owner or leave the deposit to a trusted person with the permission of the depositor. If he travels with the deposit and it is damaged or stolen, he is held liable.

Using Deposited Money for Investment

A depository may invest the deposited money with the permission of the depositor. However, he has to guarantee the return of the deposit upon demand by the depositor. As shown in Figure 6.2, the profit and the loss that may result from the investment belong to the depository. According to Maliki jurists, the profit belongs to the depository, whereas 'Abu Hanifa ruled that such profits must be given away in charity.[8] The depositor cannot demand any share of the profit unless he undertakes to suffer losses, in which case the transaction could be converted into *mudarabah,* in which the profit would be divided based on an agreed percentage and the losses would be suffered by the party who has contributed the capital.

FIGURE 6.2 Based on the principle of *wadi'ah*, a depository cannot demand a share of the profit if the depository uses the deposited money for investment purposes.

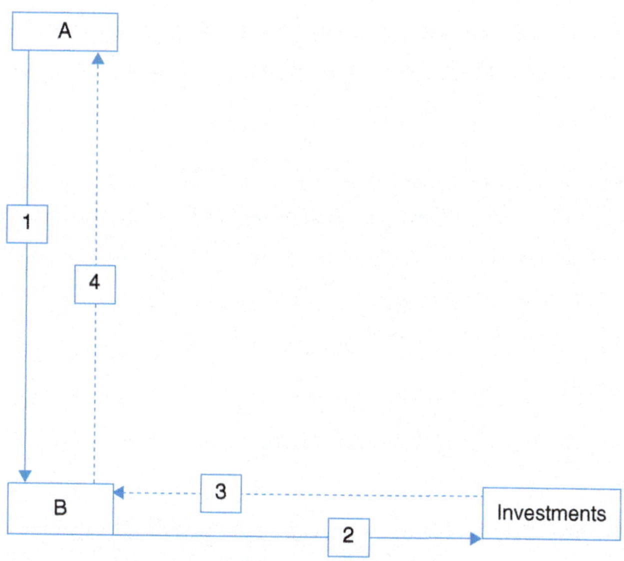

1. A deposits a certain amount of money with B.
2. B invests the money with the permission of A.
3. The principal and the profit are returned to B.
4. B returns the deposit to A upon demand.

Wadi'ah and Islamic Banks

Conventional banks accept deposits from the customers based on loan contracts. Accordingly, the relationship between a customer and a conventional bank is one that exists between a lender and a borrower. The conventional bank, which is the borrower, pays interest to the customers, who are the lenders. Borrowing money on interest is prohibited in Islam. Islamic banks, therefore, accept deposits from the customers based on a safekeeping (*wadi'ah*) contract that does not entitle the depositor to any additional amount. The resulting relationship that exists between the customers and the Islamic bank is one of a depositor and a depository. The bank seeks permission from the depositors to use and invest their money in Islamically approved investments. This changes the bank's position from a trustee to a guarantor. The customers may withdraw all or part of their deposit at any time and the bank is under an obligation to return it. The profits generated by the bank from the use of these funds belong to the bank, and, in case of loss, it is held liable. The bank provides certain facilities, such as automatic teller machines (ATMs) and checkbooks, for its customers. The bank, at its discretion, may also, from time to time, reward the customers or may give them gift (*hibah*) from the profits generated from the use of their deposited funds.

The profits generated by the bank from the use of these funds belong to the bank, and, in case of loss, it is held liable.

Gift and interest:

- Interest is contractual, whereas the provision of gift (*hibah*) is discretionary in nature. A lender stipulates that the borrower should pay interest, whereas a depositor cannot demand gift (*hibah*) and a depository is not under any obligation to provide it. However, it is prohibited if the provision of *hibah* becomes a custom.
- The provision of *hibah* is not predetermined and may reflect the performance of the business. As such, a depository may increase, decrease, or totally deny the provision of *hibah* to the depositors. In contrast, a borrower is contractually bound to give a predetermined interest to the lender without any reference to the performance of the business.
- A *hibah* can be anything like books, computers, hand phones, or cash, whereas interest is always in monetary terms.

Termination of *Wadi'ah*

The contract of safekeeping (*wadi'ah*) is a nonbinding contract. Thus, both the depositor and the depository have the right to annul the contract at any time. A *wadi'ah* contract is terminated in the following situations:

- When a depositor demands his deposit or when a depository returns the deposit.
- When either the depositor or the depository dies.

- When a depositor or a depository loses his legal capacity due to insanity or bankruptcy.
- When a depositor transfers the ownership of the deposit to another through a sale or gift contract.[9]

The Differences Between the Contracts of *Wadi'ah* and *Qard*

The following are the differences between the contracts of deposit and loan:

- In *wadi'ah* the ownership of the deposit is not transferred to the depository, whereas in *qard* the ownership of the borrowed money is transferred to the borrower.
- Because, in deposit, the ownership still remains with the depository, the depository is liable to pay *zakat* for the money he or she has deposited.
- A depository in a *wadi'ah* contract is a trustee, whereas a borrower is a guarantor.
- The depository should produce the deposit on demand, whereas a lender is recommended to give respite to a borrower who is in financial restraints.
- A loan is given to help a person in need, whereas the purpose of the *wadi'ah* contract is the safekeeping and protection of a property.
- In *wadi'ah*, a depositor may impose certain conditions on how the deposit should be kept, whereas in *qard* a lender cannot impose any conditions on the borrower.
- A depositor can withdraw the deposited money gradually, whereas a borrower is required to return the loan in lump sum.

Chapter Questions

True/False

1. ( ) A depository has to guarantee the safety of the deposited property.
2. ( ) A depository can charge the depositor for any cost that he may incur for safekeeping the deposit.
3. ( ) In a *wadi'ah* contract, the ownership of the deposited property during the period of the deposit is transferred to the depository.
4. ( ) A depository who uses the deposit is not liable for any loss or damage to the deposit.
5. ( ) If deposited money is used as capital for a business activity, the profit earned belongs to the depositor.
6. ( ) A depository may demand fees in return for keeping the deposited money.
7. ( ) A depositor who deposits money with a bank based on *wadi'ah* contract is not entitled to any share in the profit that may result from the investment of that money.

8. ( ) If a depository uses the deposited property, his position is changed from a trustee to a guarantor.
9. ( ) A depositor who deposits money with a bank, based on *wadi'ah,* should be given a share in the profit that may result from investing his money.
10. ( ) A depository who uses the deposited money is responsible for any loss.

Short Answer

1. Discuss when the status of a depository as a trustee could be changed into a guarantor.
2. Can a depositor demand a share in the profit if the depository uses the deposited money for investment purposes?
3. Can a depository use the deposited money for investment purposes?

Notes

1. See Muhammad Asad, *The Message of the Quran* (Gibraltar: Dar al-Andalus, 1980), note 75 on verse 4:58.
2. See Wahbah al-Zuhaili, *Financial Transactions in Islamic Jurisprudence,* vol. 1, 579, trans. Mahmoud A. El-Gamal (Beirut: Dar al-Fikr al-Mouaser, 2003).
3. *The Mejelle,* trans. C.R. Tyser, D. G. Demetriades, Ismail Haqqi Effendi (Petaling Jaya: The Other Press, 2001), Article 798.
4. *The Mejelle,* Articles 790–791.
5. Ibid, Article 787.
6. Ibid, Articles 788–789.
7. Ibid, Article 794.
8. Wahbah al-Zuhaili, *Financial Transactions in Islamic Jurisprudence,* vol. 1, 597.
9. Ibid, 599.

CHAPTER

7

Partnership (*al-Sharikat*)

Learning outcomes

At the end of this chapter, you should be able to:

1. Distinguish partnership from co-ownership.
2. Define the types of partnerships and their pillars and conditions.
3. Apply the various types of partnerships to different business activities.
4. Apply the concept of decreasing partnership (*musharakah mutanaqisah*) to investment activities and house financing.

Introduction

Sharikah literally means mixing of two properties in a manner that they could not be distinguished from each other. It also means sharing, and participation. It also means a property that belongs to several owners or co-proprietors in common, in such a way that each one had ownership of every smallest part of it in proportion to the share allotted to him. In a *Hadith Qudsi,* it is stated that Allah (swt) says: "I make a third with two partners as long as one of them does not cheat the other, but when he cheats him, I depart from them."[1]

أنا ثالث الشريكين ما لم يخن أحدهما صاحبه فإذا خانه خرجت من بينهما

Division of *al-Sharikat*

Generally, *al-sharikat* could be divided into two broad divisions of shared ownership and contractual partnerships, as presented in Figure 7.1.

FIGURE 7.1 Al-Sharikat is divided into two broad categories of co-ownership and contractual partnership. Contractual partnership is divided into three types: partnership of capital, partnership of services, and partnership of creditworthiness.

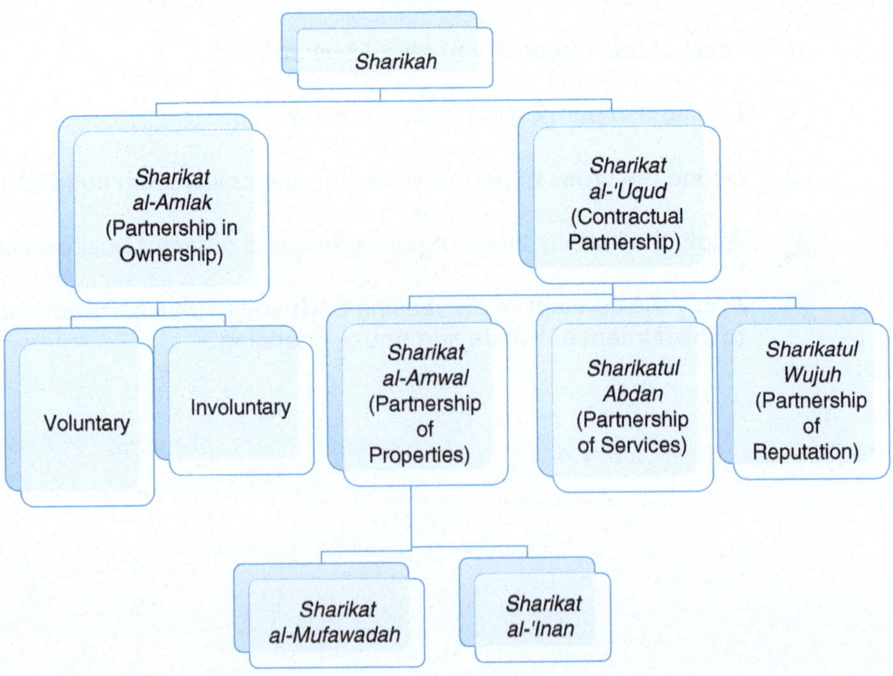

Shared Ownership or Co-Ownership (Sharikat al-Amlak)

It is a type of *sharika* in which two or more persons become joint owners of a property without entering into a partnership contract. This joint ownership could be established either by operation of law, such as through inheritance, or through other contracts such as *wasiyyah* or gift (*hibah*) or purchase. The partners have to share the property or its income based on their allotted respective shares until they decide to divide it (if it is divisible, for example, land) or to sell it (if it is indivisible, for example, a house, flat, or a car) and divide the price among them. *Sharikat al-amlak* is subdivided into voluntary and involuntary co-ownership, as shown in Figure 7.1. Voluntary partnership refers to a situation in which two or more persons jointly buy a property or receive a certain property as a gift or as a result of a will (*wasiyyah*) because, in all these cases, the acceptance of the parties is needed. Involuntary partnership refers to a situation in which two or more persons acquire the ownership over something without any action on their part. This may happen, for example, when two or more persons jointly inherit a certain property.

In *sharikat al-amlak,* a partner has no authority over another partner's share and is not allowed to interfere in the property without the other partner's permission. The essence of *sharikat al-amlak* is common ownership of property. It is not partnership in which each partner is considered an agent for the other. It has not come into existence by mutual agreement of parties in which they authorise each other over the partnership capital.

Contractual Partnership (Sharikat al-'Uqud)

It is considered a proper type of partnership because the parties concerned have willingly entered into a contractual agreement for joint investment and sharing of profits and loss. It can be defined as a contract between two or more partners in the capital and profit. The Mejelle defines partnership as an agreement for association, on the condition that the capital and its benefits are common between two or more persons.[2] According to the Hanafii jurists, partnership has two pillars of offer and acceptance. The other jurists argue that partnership has three pillars. They are the parties, the object or subject matter of the partnership, and the expression, which consists of offer and acceptance. In a contractual partnership, each partner is considered an agent for the other. In contractual partnership, the partners may contribute money/capital, reputation, or services. Based on this, a contractual partnership could be divided into the following main types, as presented in Figure 7.1:

1. Partnership of capital (*Sharikat al-Amwal*).
2. Partnership of services (*Sharikat al-A'mal/Abdan*).
3. Partnership of reputation or creditworthiness (*Sharikat al-Wujuh*).

Sharikah al-a'mal/abdan refers to a partnership among workers/professionals, whereas *sharikat al-wujuh* is a type of partnership in which partners use their creditworthiness, good name, and reputation to buy goods on credit and sell them in cash.

Capital Partnerships (*Sharikat al-Amwal*)

In capital partnership (*sharikat al-amwal*), partners contribute their capital. Capital partnership is subdivided into *sharikat al-mufawada,* and *sharikat al-'inan.*

*Equal Contribution Partnership (*Sharikat al-Mufawada*)*

Mufawada literally means equality and delegation. Technically, it refers to a partnership in which two or more persons become partners in a venture on the condition that they equally contribute to the capital and management and equally share profits or losses, as shown in Figure 7.2. All partners should have the same religion. The partners must contribute all their capital to the partnership capital, which means that neither of them must be richer than the other. Each partner is an agent as well as a guarantor (*kafeel*) for the other partners. A partner is liable for the actions

FIGURE 7.2 **A, B, and C form *sharkat al-mufawadah* by contributing the same amount of capital and sharing the profits and losses equally.**

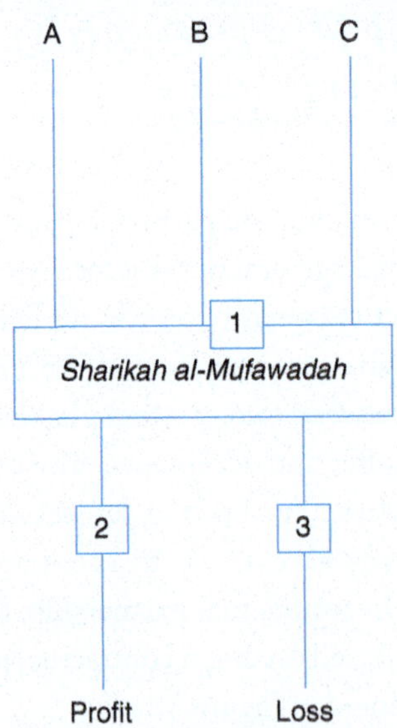

1. A, B, and C contribute equal amounts of capital to form *Sharikat al-mufawadah.*
2. They equally share the profit.
3. They equally share the loss.

of other partners, and an undertaking by one of the partner binds all other partners. The Shafi'is, Hanbalis, and Malikis do not agree with the Hanafiis version of *sharikat al-mufawadah* and argue that the exact equality required by the Hanafii jurists is almost impossible.[3] It is possible to argue that *sharikat al-mufawadah* may still be relevant to family businesses when a certain partnership is run by members of the same family.

Unequal Contribution Partnership (Sharikat al-'Inan)

It is a partnership in which two or more partners contribute different amounts of capital and share the profit and loss in different proportions. In this type of partnership, as presented in Figure 7.3, equality in the contribution of capital, in the participation in the management of the enterprise, or in the distribution of profit and loss is not a condition. One of the partners may contribute more capital than the others. It is also possible that one or more partners run the business while the rest may not participate. Partners are considered agents for each other whereby an action done by one of them in the ordinary course of business binds other partners. However, partners are not guarantors for each other, and their liabilities toward third parties outside the partnership business are individual and not joint.

FIGURE 7.3 A, B, and C contribute different amounts of money to form *sharikat al-'inan*. They share the profits and losses in different proportions.

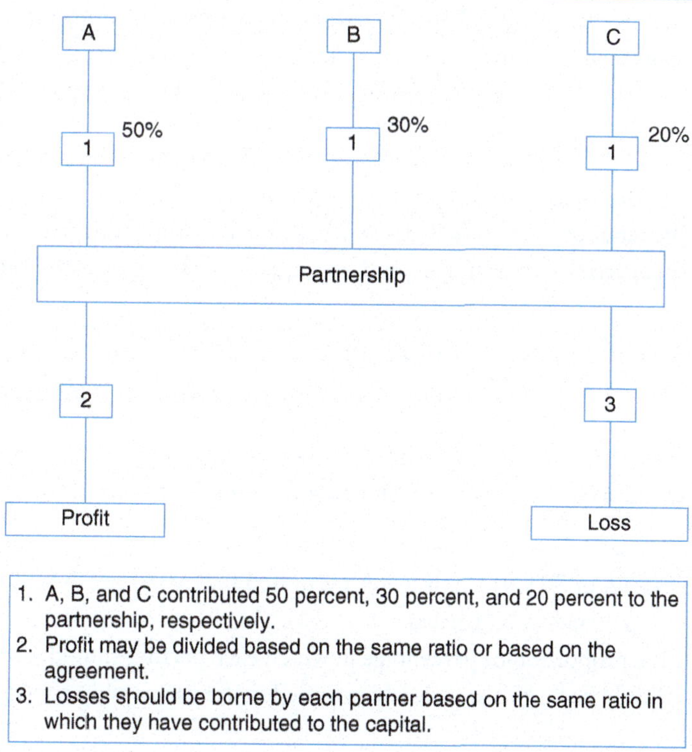

Conditions related to the capital of *sharikat al 'inan:*

- The capital should be a type of property on which agency is possible.
- The capital contributed by each partner should be known.
- The percentage in which each partner contributed his or her capital to the total capital of the partnership should be clearly ascertained, as all rights, obligations, profit, or losses are based on the ratio in which partners contribute to the capital of partnership.
- The capital contributed by each partner should be present. Debt cannot be contributed as the capital for the partnership.
- The capital contributed by each partner should be mixed together in such a way that the capital of one partner cannot be distinguished from that of the other.
- The majority of the jurists argue that the capital contributed by the partners should be in liquid form, that is, in cash. They oppose contribution in kind on the ground that an asset contributed by a partner is always distinguishable from the asset contributed by the other partners. For example, if A contributes in cash and B contributes a car, the properties cannot be mixed together. A may remain the owner of the money and B the owner of the vehicle. The Maliki jurists, however, are of the opinion that liquidity of the capital is not a condition of the partnership. They argue that it is permissible if a partner contributes in kind. In this case, his share in the partnership capital will be determined based on the market price of the property at the time when it is contributed. They also argue that all partners become co-owners of the combined capital, irrespective of whether they have contributed in cash or in kind. Thus, the parties may contribute in cash or assets such as land, building, machinery, and equipment, which are suitable for the partnership. These assets will be registered at their market value as the share of a particular partner who contributes them. Accordingly, all partners would become co-owners of the liquid money and fixed assets in accordance with their ratio in the total capital irrespective of who paid in cash and who paid in kind.

The Shafi'i jurists are of the opinion that partners may contribute homogeneous properties to the partnership capital. Based on this argument, contribution in the form of homogeneous properties such as oil, wheat, or rice could be accepted, whereas nonhomogeneous properties such as house, land, or car cannot form part of the *Musharakah* capital.

The capital contributed by each partner should be present. Debt cannot be contributed as the capital for a partnership.

Conditions for the distribution of profit and loss in *sharikat al 'inan:*

- The profit must be assigned to the partners based on percentage or proportions such as 20, 30, or 50 percent. It is not permitted that a partner should receive a specific amount of money such as RM 5,000.
- The proportion or percentage in which each partner should receive his or her share of profit should be known and clearly specified in the partnership contract.

- Each partner should receive his or her specified proportion or percentage of the actual profit gained by the business.
- According to the Maliki and Shafi'i jurists, each partner should receive the profit exactly in the same percentage in which he or she has contributed to the partnership capital. For instance, if a partner has contributed 40 percent of the partnership capital, he must also receive 40 percent of the profit. According to them, any condition that entitles him to more or less than 40 percent is invalid. These schools argue that the share of a partner in profit and loss must conform to the ratio of his investment. According to the Hanafii and Hanbali jurists, on the other hand, the ratio of the profit may differ from the ratio of investment and could be decided based on the agreement between the partners. There may be a situation in which some of the partners may not contribute to the entrepreneurship and management of the partnership. In this case, profit need not be shared in accordance with the capital contribution. It may be shared in any proportion agreed by the partners, depending on their contributions to the success and profitability of the business.
- All Muslim jurists are unanimous that each partner shall suffer the loss exactly according to the same ratio in which he or she has contributed to the partnership capital.

Management of Partnership (*Sharikat al-'Inan*)

Every partner has the right to take part in the management of the partnership. However, partners may also agree that the business should be run by one or some of them, and no other partners shall work for the partnership. The partners who manage the partnership act as agents for the other partners. Thus, all rights and obligation that may arise in the ordinary course of business are attributed to all the partners and not only to those who are running the business.

A partner or partners who are entrusted with the management of the business are considered trustees (*amin*). As a trustee, he or she is not legally liable for the losses if they occur in the normal course of running the business. However, if he or she intentionally transgresses the partnership property, performs his or her duties negligently, or goes beyond the terms of the contract, he or she will be personally held responsible.

Partnership of Services (*Sharikat al-a'mal*)

Partnership of services (*Sharikat al-a'mal*, also known as *Sharikat al-abdan* or *Sharikat al Sanai'*) refers to a partnership of two or more workers/professionals who agree to contribute their labour/service to a joint enterprise and share the earnings. The partners only contribute their labour, service, and skills without contributing to the capital. They jointly undertake to render some services for their customers, and the fee charged from them is distributed among the partners according to an agreed ratio.

The Shafi'i jurists have argued that the partnership of services is not valid because of the absence of capital contribution by the partners. They argue that the labour and service contributed by the parties cannot form the capital of partnership. Furthermore, the contribution of labour and services by the partners cannot be quantified. Consequently, they argue that the partnership suffers from ambiguity (*gharar*), as the exact percentage in which the partners contribute their labour or service is not known. Consequently sharing of profit among the partners would lead to injustice. They therefore prefer that each person should individually work and earn his profit. The Hanafii, Maliki, and Hanbali jurists, on the other hand, argue that the purpose of the parties in a partnership of services is to collect profit for which partners may become agents to each other. They also argue that human beings since time immemorial used partnership of services to jointly undertake the performance of a certain task that was difficult for a single individual to perform. Moreover, they contend that labour could become the capital of partnership by an analogy to a *mudarabah* partnership, whereas a *mudarib* only contributes his efforts and labour.[4]

In practice, *sharikat al-a'mal* could be concluded, for instance, between two or more tailors, plumbers, shoe-makers, barbers, lawyers, physicians, dentists, or accountants who agree to contribute their labour/services and skills in order to jointly undertake and perform a certain task and to share the income among them either equally or based on an agreement.

Moreover, certain enterprises require a combination of different skills and expertise. For instance, a partner may contribute his creative skill of drawing and fashion to create a design, another may contribute his sewing skill to make the dress, and another partner may contribute his marketing skill to sell the clothes. Similarly, experts from marketing and pharmaceutical sciences may come together to sell a new type of herbal medicines. Another example, as presented in Figure 7.4, is a tuition centre in which teachers specialised in different fields such as mathematics, physics, chemistry, and biology agree to form a partnership and teach the same students different courses. Even nonskilled workers may undertake to jointly do certain physical work and share the revenue among them.

Sharikah al-a'mal is a way to empower the worker or professionals to come together, form a partnership, jointly perform tasks, and share the revenue instead of being employed by an employer for doing the same job in return for wages/salaries. *Sharikah al-a'mal* encourages the workers/professionals to jointly form enterprises/businesses, even if there is no capital.

Partnership of Reputation or Creditworthiness (*Sharikat al-Wujuh*)

Wujuh refers to goodwill, creditworthiness, and good reputation. In partnership of creditworthiness, two or more persons agree to purchase goods upon their personal credit (without immediately paying the price) and to sell them through their joint efforts on their joint account. The partners do not contribute any capital. Partners purchase commodities at a lower deferred price and sell them for cash. They may share the profit either equally or based on an agreed ratio.

FIGURE 7.4 A, B, and C jointly establish a tuition centre, teach different subjects, and share the revenue based on the agreement.

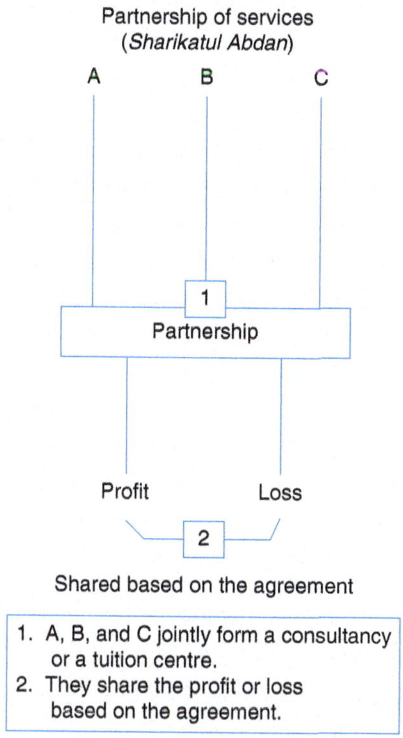

Partners may own unequal amount of goods, and, in this case, profit and loss must be determined based on the partners, share in the ownership of the goods.[5]

Sharikat al-wujuh allows each partner to purchase various types of goods, which can subsequently increase the quantity of the goods purchased, which, in turn, results in more sales and greater income to the partners. It allows the partners to create wealth/make profit without contributing to the initial capital. For example, two or more retailers may purchase goods from several wholesalers on credit and jointly sell them for cash, as shown in Figure 7.5. Similarly, two or more companies may combine their goodwill and reputation to purchase goods from the manufacturers or bulk suppliers on credit for a lower price and sell them to their customers.

Sharikat al-wujuh would benefit individuals and companies that do not have sufficient capital to purchase goods in cash. This also encourages individuals and companies to establish their goodwill, which, in turn, would benefit the society at large. *Sharikat al-wujuh* is encouraging suppliers to sell goods on credit instead of making purchasers to borrow cash from others and use the money to buy goods from the suppliers in cash.

For example, two or more students may form a partnership of creditworthiness (*sharikat al-wujuh*) by agreeing to purchase various types of clothes or books on credit for a lower price. Each of them will buy from wholesalers or publishers on a deferred basis, based on his/her personal creditworthiness and good reputation. They then will jointly sell the clothes or

FIGURE 7.5 A, B, and C purchase goods from the suppliers on credit, sell them in cash, and share the profits based on the agreement.

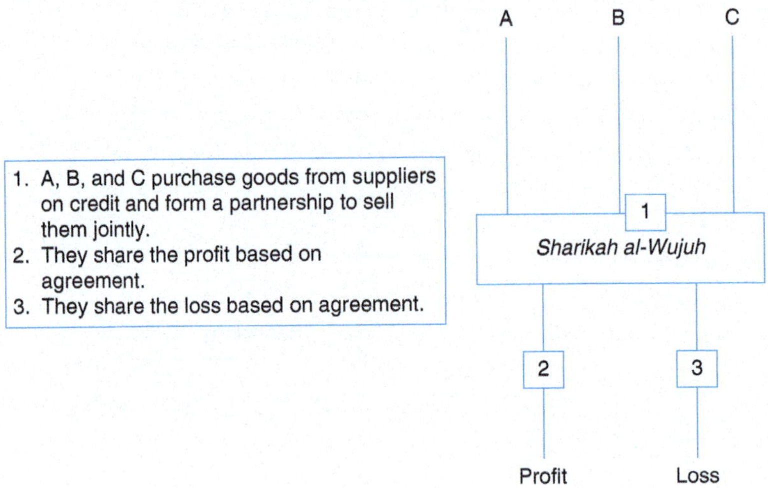

books to the students at the university. After the goods are sold, they will pay the outstanding amount to the wholesalers, and the balance is the profit for them. The profit will be distributed according to the agreement or based on goods purchased and contributed by each partner.

Partnership (*Sharikat al-'Inan/Musharakah*) and Islamic Banks

Islam has termed interest as an unjust instrument of financing and prohibited its use for providing funds. Lending at a fixed, predetermined interest rate favours the lender and is not concerned with the success of the venture he finances. One of the alternatives to the interest-based financing is partnership (*sharikat/musharakah*). In *musharakah,* instead of lending money at a fixed rate of return, an Islamic bank forms a partnership with the customer, sharing in a venture's profit and losses. Whereas interest is a predetermined fixed return, the return in *musharakah* is based on the actual profit earned by a joint venture. An Islamic bank is not merely a lender but an investor who has a stake in the success of the business. *Musharakah* also allows a capital-poor but promising entrepreneur to obtain financing.

Islamic banks may use partnership (*sharikat al-'inan* or *musharakah*) to finance imports and exports. A trader may approach an Islamic bank for partial financing for a single transaction of importing goods. After the goods are sold, the trader and the bank may share the profit according to a pre-agreed ratio. Partnership can also be used to finance exports of goods. For example, a trader who has a specific order from abroad may approach an Islamic bank for partial financing for a single transaction of exporting goods. The price of the exported goods is known in advance, and the bank can easily calculate the expected profit. The partner may manage the partnership, and, in return, he or she would be entitled to a percentage of the profit. Alternatively, both the bank and the client may jointly manage the business or they may choose to appoint an executive body to manage it. The bank may reserve the right to supervise the management. Throughout the period of partnership, both the bank and the client stay as partners. The partnership does not end with the ownership of the client.

Decreasing Partnership (Musharakah Mutanaqisah)

The bank and a customer may enter into a *musharakah* contract to finance certain investment activity or a project. Each partner will contribute to the capital of this activity with a certain percentage. As soon as the activity starts and profits are realised, one of the two partners (the bank), may withdraw gradually from the project by selling its shares to the other partner. The share of the bank in the profits will be diminished in the same proportion in which its ownership share in the partnership is reduced, while the share of the other partner in both the project and the profits will increase at the same time. The partner has the option to purchase the ownership units/shares and he or she cannot be forced to buy them. The price for which the shares are purchased is negotiable and should be based on the market price. The bank may benefit from this type of *musharakah* by making a profit, and the entrepreneur acquires a productive enterprise, which may be developed or expanded.

Decreasing Partnership (Musharakah Mutanaqisah) *for Home Financing*

In this case an Islamic bank and a customer jointly purchase a house. The customer may contribute 10 percent of the capital needed for the purchase of the house while the bank contributes the other 90 percent. Once the house is purchased, it will be leased to the customer. The bank should not charge rentals for the period when the house is still under construction and is not ready for residence. The rentals could only be charged when the house comes to the possession of the customer. This will distinguish house rentals from interest paid on loan. The customer pays the monthly rental to the bank for its 90 percent share in the ownership of the house. The amount of rental could be determined with reference to the rental market of the locality. The bank should not unilaterally decide or change the rental amount, as the customer is a co-owner of the house.

Meanwhile the customer (the partner) has the option to purchase ownership units/shares from the bank. He may purchase some or all of the ownership shares. Monthly payment to the bank includes rental and the purchase price of the ownership units. The price the partner pays for the purchase of the shares should be determined by the market value of the property at the time of sale. The ownership shares/units should be sold for the market value. If the market value of the house rises or falls, it should also affect the price of the shares. As the customer gradually acquires more ownership units, the amount of rental payable to the bank is reduced. This will continue until the customer acquires 100 percent ownership of the house. In decreasing partnership, the bank and the customer are partners and not creditor and debtor, as is the case with the *Bay Bi-thaman Ajil* (BBA) or conventional mortgage.

In decreasing partnership, the bank and the customer are partners and not creditor and debtor, as is the case with the Bay Bi-thaman Ajil *(BBA) or conventional mortgage.*

Decreasing partnership (*musharakah mutanaqisa* [MM]) house-financing facility is currently proposed as a potential alternative to replace the much criticised BBA contract. The following are the main differences between MM house-financing facility and BBA.

- BBA involves *bay' al-'einah,* whereas MM avoids *bay' al-'einah* by making the bank and the customer partners and joint owners.
- BBA creates debt on the customer, whereas MM is a joint ownership in which the customer purchases ownership units from the bank.
- In case of default or early redemption, BBA is more costly, whereas MM is a joint investment that may come to an end in a normal way. In case of repossession, both parties will share the price of the house.
- In BBA, the bank does not take any risk if a housing project is abandoned, because the customer initially buys and owns the house. In MM, both the bank and the customer as co-owners jointly take the risk of abandoned projects.

MM house financing facility is also different from conventional mortgage as follows:

- MM is a joint investment, whereas a conventional mortgage is an interest-based loan.
- In MM, rental is paid, whereas in a conventional mortgage, interest is paid.
- In case of default, both partners can recover their share when the house is sold, but in a conventional mortgage, the house will go for foreclosure and the bank will recover principal and interest.

Dissolution of Partnership

Partnership is a nonbinding contract. However, partners may agree to make a binding partnership agreement for a certain period. A partnership may come to an end in the following circumstances:

- When a partnership fulfils its objective or when its duration is expired.
- By mutual consent of the partners.
- By a request made by one of the partners, which is subsequently approved by other partners.
- By death or incapacity of one of the parties whose heirs or their guardian decide to discontinue the partnership.
- By the bankruptcy of the partners or one of them.

In case of liquidation, the assets of the partnership will be liquidated to enable the partners to know the gross as well as the net position of the *musharakah* enterprise. In case of liquidation:

- The outstanding obligation of the partnership is discharged first.
- The capital shares are paid next.
- If profit is realised, it should be distributed in accordance with the terms of the contract.
- In case of loss, the parties will bear the loss in the same ratio in which they contributed to the partnership capital. The losses are paid first out of the profit made by the partnership. If there is no profit or the profit made is not enough to cover the losses, then the capital of the partnership is used to pay for the losses. However, if the capital is not sufficient to cover the losses, the partners must pay, in proportion to their shares in the capital, out of their own private means.

Chapter Questions

True/False

1. ( ) In a partnership contract (*sharikatul-'inan*), a partner can contribute his management skill and expertise but not the capital.
2. ( ) In a partnership (*sharkat al-'inan*), the liabilities of the partners are not limited to their contribution to the capital.
3. ( ) In a partnership (*shariak al-'inan*), partners may decide by an agreement on the distribution of losses.
4. ( ) All Muslim jurists agree that the capital in a partnership (*sharikat al-'inan*) should be in cash.
5. ( ) In a decreasing partnership (*musharakah mutanaqisah*), an Islamic bank may gradually buy the share of the entrepreneur.
6. ( ) A partner who also manages the partnership may receive a certain fixed remuneration for his efforts.
7. ( ) In *sharikat al-wujuh,* two professionals become partners and agree to work and share their earnings.
8. ( ) In *sharikat al-a'mal,* two persons who possess no property become partners by agreeing to purchase goods jointly upon their personal credit.

9. ( ) *Sharikat al-amlak* is a type of partnership that may come into existence by operation of law.
10. ( ) In *sharikat al-amlak,* one partner is considered an agent for another partner.

Short Answer

1. Explain in which ways co-ownership (*sharikat al-amlak*) differs from contractual partnership (*sharikat al'uqud*).
2. Discuss how profit and loss is distributed in a partnership (*sharikat al-'inan*) contract.
3. Islamic banks may use decreasing partnership (*musharakah mutanaqisa*) to enable a customer to own a house.
   a. Briefly discuss the various contracts that are included in a *musharakah mutanaqisa* financing facility.
   b. How does *musharakah mutanaqisa* enable an Islamic bank to make profit and enable its customer to own a house?
4. A person is willing to act as a partner and provide 50 percent of the capital you need for your business enterprise. Suggest any possible business plan/proposal for the partnership (*musharakah*). Your proposal must include the following:
   a. The type of the business you want to set up, the amount of total capital needed for the business, and the profit and loss sharing ratio between the partners.
   b. How losses would be dealt with.
   c. How the partnership would come to an end and the capital returned to the partners.
5. Discuss the following contractual partnerships and show their applications by providing relevant examples.
   a. The partnership of services (*sharikah al-abdan*).
   b. The partnership of reputation/creditworthiness (*sharika al-wujuh*).
6. Ahmad, Zaid, and Lutfi have agreed to form a partnership. Ahmad contributed RM 50,000, Zaid RM 30,000, and Lutfi RM 20,000. They decided to buy medicine from pharmaceutical companies and supply them to pharmacies. Ahmad and Zaid are overseas and Lutfi, who is a skilled pharmacist, runs and manages the business. Ahmad and Zaid agreed that Lutfi should receive a salary of RM 3,000 per month from the partnership. They also agreed that Lutfi should also receive 50 percent of the profit. Ahmad would receive 30 percent, and Zaid would receive 20 percent of the profit. Discuss the following:
   a. Critically examine the profit-sharing ratio among the partners based on juristic opinions of the various *Fiqh* schools.
   b. Discuss how the partners would have to share the losses.
   c. Explain what steps should be taken in case of liquidation when the partnership would come to an end.

Notes

1. Sunan Abu Dawud, Book 22, no. 3377, Imam Albani considers the hadith weak. See his al-Irwa, no. 1468 and Da'eef al-Jami' al-Sagheer, no. 1748.
2. *The Mejelle*, trans. C.R. Tyser, D. G. Demetriades, Ismail Haqqi Effendi (Petaling Jaya: The Other Press, 2001), Article 1329.
3. See Wahbah al-Zuhaili, *Financial Transactions in Islamic Jurisprudence*, vol. 1, 451–452.
4. Ibid, 455–456.
5. Ibid, 454.

CHAPTER 8

Silent Partnership (*Mudarabah/Qirad*)

Learning outcomes

At the end of this chapter, you should be able to:

1. Define the pillars and main conditions of a *mudarabah* contract.
2. Understand the rights and obligations of the *sahib al-mal* and the *mudarib*, issues related to the sharing of profit, and the treatment of loss.
3. Explain the types of *mudarabah* contract, the acts that a *mudarib* cannot perform without the permission of the *sahib al-mal,* and void *mudarabah* contracts.
4. Apply the various types of *mudarabah* to different business activities.
5. Compare and contrast *mudarabah* and *musharakah* partnership contracts.

Introduction

Mudarabah is derived from the Arabic word *daraba,* which means travelling for trade. *Mudarabah* refers to a contract in which one of the parties provides capital (*sahib al-mal*) and the other contributes expertise, labour, and entrepreneurial skill (*mudarib*) to conduct a particular business in which both parties would share profit. The model is presented in Figure 8.1. There are people who have capital but either do not have time or do not know how or where to invest it. There are others who have the entrepreneurial skills and business acumen but have no capital. *Mudarabah* enables both parties to make profit. The owner of the capital benefits from the experience and skills of the *mudarib,* and the *mudarib* benefits from the capital that he invests in a profitable way. Both parties share the profit. The loss is first offset by the profit, and if the profit is not enough, it is taken from the capital of the *mudarabah.*

The practice of *mudarabah* was common among the pre-Islamic Arabs. The Prophet (pbAbuh) himself entered into a *mudarabah* contract with Khadijah (mAbpwh). After the advent of Islam, *mudarabah* was approved and continued to be practised. Caliph Umar (mAbpwh) and other companions used to invest the properties of the orphans in *mudarabah* businesses so that *zakat* would not reduce the wealth of the orphans.

FIGURE 8.1 **The parties enter into a *mudarabah* contract and agree to share the profit and loss proportionally based on the agreement. Profit should be used to offset losses, and if there is no sufficient profit to cover losses, they should be borne by the *sahib al-mal.***

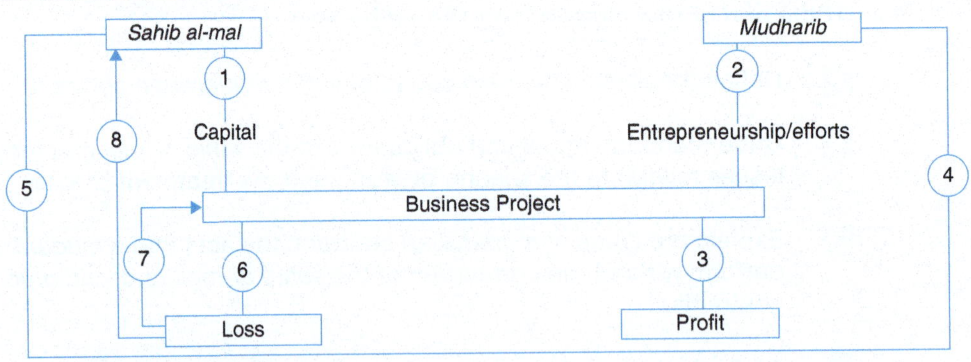

1. *Sahib al-mal* contributes the capital.
2. *Mudarib* contributes the efforts.
3. Profit made.
4. The share of the *mudarib* in the profit.
5. The share of the *sahib al-mal* int he profit.
6. Losses made.
7. Losses are offset by the profit from the business.
8. If losses are more than profit, they are borne by the *sahib al-mal.*

Pillars of *Mudarabah* Contract

According to the Hanafiis, *mudarabah* has two pillars of offer and acceptance. *Mudarabah* is concluded when the parties use words that clearly indicate the contract of *mudarabah* in their offer and acceptance. According to the majority of the *Fiqh* schools, the contract of *mudarabah* has three pillars. They are the parties that consist of the owner of the capital (*sahib al-mal*) and the entrepreneur or the manager (*mudarib* or *'aamil*); the subject matter of the contract, which includes the capital, the efforts, and the profit; and expression, which is made of offer and acceptance. According to the Shafi'i scholars, *mudarabah* has five pillars. They are the contracting parties, the capital, the work, the profit, and expression, which includes offer and acceptance.

A *sahib al-mal* may contract *mudarabah* with more than one person through a single transaction. The capital can be utilised by these *mudaribs* jointly, and the share of the *mudarib* shall be distributed between them according to the agreed proportion. An entrepreneur may also become a *mudarib* for many investors in the business.

Conditions pertaining to the capital of *mudarabah* include:

- The capital provider (*sahib al-mal*) and the entrepreneur (*mudarib*) should be eligible to assume the role of a principal and an agent, respectively. The *sahib al-mal* must own the capital of the *mudarabah*, as the entrepreneur, while investing the capital of the *sahib al-mal*, represents him.
- The capital should be in liquid or cash form, such as dinar, dirham, or currencies that are commonly in circulation. According to the majority of the Muslim jurists, the capital of a *mudarabah* should not be in kind in the form of goods or commodities, as their prices may fluctuate. They argue that in such cases the initial value of the *mudarabah* capital may not be known and can only be estimated. Thus, there exists ambiguity (*gharar*) as to the real amount of capital and subsequently as to the amount of profit made. At liquidity it may lead to disputes between the parties over the amount of capital and profit, as profit refers to any addition over the principal. However, it is permissible if a *sahib al-mal* gives goods and other properties to a *mudarib* and instructs him to sell them and use the price as the capital of the *mudarabah*. In this case the capital of the *mudarabah* is not the goods and properties, but their price, which is known. In contrast, according to Imam al-Awza'i and Ibn Abi Layla, the *sahib al-mal* may contribute in kind or non-monetary capital provided the price of the goods is known at the time when the *mudarabah* contract is concluded. This, they argue, removes the possibility of *gharar*.[1]
- The amount of the capital should be known. It is important, as it leads to a clear distinction between the capital and the profit, as profit refers to any additional amount over and above the capital.
- The capital should be present. It is, for instance, not allowed for a creditor to enter into a *mudarabah* with his debtor.
- The capital should be delivered to *mudarib* and come to his complete possession. This is to enable a *mudarib* to use the capital and to establish his status as a trustee.

The Status of *Sahib al-mal* and *Mudarib*

A *sahib al-mal* who provides capital to a *mudarib* is not a lender, as the ownership of the invested money still remains with him. Similarly, a *mudarib* is not a borrower. He is an agent of the *sahib al-mal* and a trustee of the *mudarabah* assets. He is not obliged to provide collateral. A *mudarib* neither guarantees to the investor the return of his capital nor the profit. In any investment there is always the possibility of loss and it is not within the power of a *mudarib* to avoid it. However, a *mudarib* should take all possible steps to minimise the risk of loss. Similarly, it is not permissible to guarantee to the *sahib al-mal* a fixed rate of profit in advance. A *mudarabah* contract, in substance, will be an interest-bearing loan if a capital provider is guaranteed his capital and a fixed profit in advance.

A *mudarib* is not held responsible if a *mudarabah* business suffers losses. His statement accompanied by oath should be accepted unless negligence or mismanagement on his part is proven. However, a *mudarib* is expected to exert due diligence, and all business dealings must be characterised by transparency. The *mudarib* should not misrepresent and give fraudulent information about the venture. He is under duty to inform the investor if the funds are in grave condition and at risk of loss. A *sahib al-mal*, on his part, must ensure that the *mudarib* has a good track record, is experienced, and enjoys high moral standing within the business community. He must also ensure that the business project is viable and assessed independently by the *sahib al-mal* or by the external consultants. The *sahib al-mal* must also ensure that the *mudarabah* venture is properly monitored.

The liability of a *sahib al-mal* in a *mudarabah* contract is limited to the extent of his capital like that of a shareholder of a limited company. Hence, a *mudarib* is not allowed to commit the *mudarabah* business to any sum greater than the capital of the *mudarabah* except with the permission of the *sahib al-mal*.

The liability of a sahib al-mal *in a* mudarabah *contract is limited to the extent of his capital like that of a shareholder of a limited company.*

Distribution of Profit and Treatment of Losses

Mudarabah is not valid if the distribution of profit between the *sahib al-mal* and *mudarib* is not clearly determined. The distribution of profit between a *sahib al-mal* and *mudarib* should be clearly defined on the basis of percentage or proportionality, such as 40, 50, or 70 percent. It is not allowed to agree on a fixed return to either the *sahib al-mal* or the *mudarib*. A fixed return and a guaranteed capital to the *sahib al-mal* will change the *mudarabah* into an interest-based loan. A fixed return to the *mudarib* will change the *mudarabah* into an employment contract. Hence, a *mudarib* cannot claim any periodical salary or a fee for his service. He is only entitled to share the profit with the *sahib al-mal*.

Profit refers to any additional amount over and above the principal capital. The Prophet (pbAbuh) is reported to have said: "the example of a person who offers prayers (*salat*) is like that of a merchant. The latter may not receive his profits until he delivers the principal capital, and the former is not rewarded for supererogatory deeds until he performs all obligatory acts of worships."[2]

مثل التاجر، لا يخلص له ربحه حتى يأخذ رأس ماله، فكذلك المصلي لا يقبل له صلاة نافلة حتى يؤدي الفريضة مثل المصلي

Accordingly, distribution of profit in *mudarabah* can only take place after the losses have been written off and the capital of the *sahib al-mal* has been fully restored. The balance, if any, is considered profit and would be distributed between the parties in accordance with the agreed ratio.[3]

Profit refers to any additional amount over and above the principal capital.

Distribution of profit could be done in one stroke at the end of the *mudarabah* contract or periodically, such as quarterly or annually, depending upon circumstances and the understanding of the parties. If profit is distributed periodically, a percentage of the profit should be used to build reserves to offset automatically any loss that may be incurred in the future. Any distribution of profit before *mudarabah* comes to an end is considered as an advance taken from the profit.

Mudarabah is a loss-absorbing contract, as presented in Figure 8.1. Upon liquidation, if a loss has been incurred in one period or investment and profit is made in another period or investment, the profit should be used to offset the losses until the entire losses have been written off. If profit is not enough to offset losses, they must be paid for out of the capital. The losses should be solely borne by the *sahib al-mal* and should not be charged to the *mudarib*, provided the losses did not result due to his negligence. Any condition that makes the *mudarib* liable for the losses or distributes losses between the parties is void.

Moral hazard in *mudarabah* may arise when a *mudarib* under-represents the profit. This problem can be mitigated by requesting periodical reports from the *mudarib*.

Types of *Mudarabah*

According to the Hanafii and Hanbali schools of *Fiqh*, *mudarabah* can be either restricted or unrestricted. The *sahib al-mal* may specify a particular business for the *mudarib*, or he may leave it open for the *mudarib* to undertake whatever business he wishes. An unrestricted *mudarabah* is a type of *mudarabah* where no restrictions concerning persons from whom the *mudarib* has to buy and to whom he has to sell, time, place, or type of trade are imposed on the *mudarib*.

Restricted *mudarabah*, on the other hand, is a type of *mudarabah* where a *mudarib's* choices concerning trading parties, place, type of business, type of properties, etc. are restricted. According to these schools, if a *sahib al-mal* imposes certain conditions, a *mudarib* is not allowed to violate them. For instance, an investor may stipulate that the capital should be invested in a particular trade, or that the trade should only be made in a particular place or only with certain persons. In case of a violation, the *mudarib* will be held liable.

The Maliki and Shafi'i jurists, on the other hand, say that *mudarabah* should not be restricted to a certain place, time, and type of trade or to certain trading partners. They argue that imposing such restrictions will limit the *mudarib's* choices and may result in certain disabilities for him. This, they say, also disagrees with the original purpose of the *mudarabah*, where the capital is entrusted to the *mudarib* to be invested in his discretion.

The advantage of imposing restrictions could be that the *mudarib* will not invest in high-risk ventures. The disadvantage could be that the *sahib al-mal* may be extremely cautious and require the *mudarib* to engage only in low-risk businesses, which could yield low profit. Consequently, the *mudarabah* business will be limited to only a handful of activities. Business will not expand, and the growth rate will be very low. Moreover, the *mudarib* will not be able to use his full potential, knowledge, and creativity to build a successful business and make profit. Imposing restrictions would limit the *mudarib's* activities and may turn him to a keeper of capital, which could be detrimental to the business.

The advantage of imposing restrictions could be that the mudarib *will not invest in high-risk ventures. The disadvantage could be that the* sahib al-mal *may be extremely cautious and require the* mudarib *to engage only in low-risk businesses, which could yield low profit.*

Personal Expenses of the *Mudarib*

A *mudarib* cannot charge his personal expenses, such as the cost of food and dwelling, to the *mudarabah* fund. According to Imam Shafi'i, an entrepreneur (*mudarib*) is only entitled to his share in the profit. If a *mudarib* charges his personal expenses to the *mudarabah* fund, it could be viewed as an extra benefit to him. Moreover, the *mudarib's* personal expenses may equal the total profits and in some cases may even exceed the total profit, in which case he would have effectively taken part of the capital.[4] Any other cost that is incurred on matters related to the *mudarabah* business, such as travelling cost, could be charged to the *mudarabah*. The Hanbali jurists argue that the *mudarib's* personal expenses related to food could be charged to *mudarabah* business if it is stipulated in the *mudarabah* contract.[5] The majority of the *Fiqh* schools restrict this right only to a situation where a *mudarib* is on a business trip. Any other expenses incurred by a *mudarib* that are acceptable in the commercial customs (*'urftijari*) could be charged to the *mudarabah* business. A *mudarib's* eligible expenses should first be charged to the profit; if there is not enough profit or no profit at all, they should be deducted from the capital of the *mudarabah*.

What the *Mudarib* Cannot Do

A *mudarib* may be authorised to do anything which is normally done in the ordinary course of business. However, he is not allowed to perform the following activities unless he obtains a clear approval or permission from the capital owner. If a *mudarib* performs any of the following activities without obtaining the permission of the capital owner, then he will be liable for any losses that may inflict the capital.

- A *mudarib* should not use the capital of the *mudarabah* to act as a *sahib al-mal* in another *mudarabah* contract. According to the Hanafii jurists, if profit is made, it has to be first distributed between the *sahib al-mal* and the first *mudarib* based on the agreement. The first *mudarib* would have to share his portion with the second *mudarib* in accordance with the agreement between them. In case of any loss, the first *mudarib* is held liable and he has to guarantee the capital, as the second *mudarib* is using the capital without the capital owner's permission. The Maliki jurists argue that since the first *mudarib* did not work for the *mudarabah* business, he is not entitled to any share in the profit based on the first *mudarabah* contract. Accordingly, the *sahib al-mal* and the second *mudarib* should share the profit. The second *mudarib* then should share his portion of the profit with the first *mudarib* based on their agreement. They also argue that in case of loss the first *mudarib* has to guarantee the capital if he enters into a *mudarabah* contract with the second *mudarib*. According to the Shafi'i jurists, the first *mudarib* is not permitted to enter into a *mudarabah* contract with a second *mudarib* with or without the permission of the *sahib al-mal*.[6]
- A *mudarib* also should not use the capital of the *mudarabah* to enter into a partnership (*sharikah/musharakah*) contract with others. He also should not mix the capital of the *mudarabah* with his own or with another person's capital and invest them.
- A *mudarib* should not purchase goods on a deferred basis. A *mudarib* also should not buy goods the total cost of which exceeds the *mudarabah* capital, as this will increase the liability of the *sahib al-mal* without his permission.
- A *mudarib* is not allowed to incur debts in the name of *mudarabah* for the purposes of *mudarabah* business. He also should not lend the capital of *mudarabah* or part of it to others.
- The *mudarib* is not allowed to commit the *mudarabah* business for any sum greater than the capital contributed by the *sahib al-mal*. The liability of the *sahib al-mal* in a *mudarabah* contract is limited to the extent of his capital contribution.

Void *Mudarabah*

According to the majority of the *Fiqh* schools, *mudarabah* is not valid if, for instance, A gives a car to B to use as a taxi, and the fare received from the passengers is distributed between them at an agreed proportion. The *mudarabah* is not valid since the taxi is not considered as valid capital for the *mudarabah*. According to the Hanafii, Shafi'i, and Hanbali, jurists the *sahib al-mal* and the *mudarib* are not bound to observe the rules of the *mudarabah* contract. They argue that this arrangement in substance falls under employment (*ijarah*) contract and not *mudarabah*. In this case, all the income that may be generated from the taxi would go to the owner of the taxi, and the driver—the employee—should be paid the going market wage for his work.

According to the Maliki jurists, a *mudarabah* contract is void if the *sahib al-mal* is guaranteed his capital against all losses even if they occur without any negligence on the part of the *mudarib*. In such a case, they argue that the *mudarabah* is void and the *mudarib* is entitled to his share of the profit, if there is any, based on the standard *mudarabah* rule. The Maliki jurists also argue that any of the following conditions stipulated by a *sahib al-mal* would make the *mudarabah* void and entitle the *mudarib* to the going market wage that is normally paid in similar circumstances to an employee.

- If a *mudarabah* contract is concluded for a fixed period such as one year.
- If a *sahib al-mal* stipulates that he would jointly manage the business with the *mudarib*.
- If a *sahib al-mal* stipulates that the *mudarib* should consult him for all the transactions.
- If a *sahib al-mal* appoints a supervisor over the *mudarib*.[7]

Termination of *Mudarabah*

A *mudarabah* contract is terminated in the following situations:

- *Mudarabah* is terminated when it is cancelled or when a *mudarib* is prevented from using the fund, or when he is dismissed. In this case, the *mudarib* is entitled to his claim in the profit. If the capital is in the form of goods, cancellation of *mudarabah*, prevention of *mudarib*, or his dismissal can only take effect after the goods are sold. The *mudarib* has to sell the goods so that the equity of the *sahib al-mal* is restored and the amount of profit is known. There is an agreement among the Muslim jurists that in this case the *mudarib* cannot be prevented from selling the goods. The cancellation, prevention, and dismissal have to be brought to the attention of the *mudarib*. The action of the *mudarib* who is unaware of the cancellation, prevention, or dismissal is binding on the *sahib al-mal*.
- If a *mudarabah* is concluded for a fixed period, it comes to an end at the expiry of that period. This is in accordance with the Hanafiis, and Hanbalis, ruling that permits fixed time *mudarabah* contract.[8]
- *Mudarabah* is terminated if either of the parties loses his legal capacity.
- *Mudarabah* is terminated when a *mudarib* in a restricted *mudarabah* does not observe one of the conditions.
- *Mudarabah* is terminated when a *mudarib* fails in his duties, and his failure is willful, intentional, and out of his negligence. In case of any loss, the *mudarib* is held liable.
- *Mudarabah* is terminated when the capital is destroyed or lost in the hands of the *mudarib*. If the destruction is caused by his negligence, the *mudarib* is held liable.
- *Mudarabah* also comes to an end when either of the parties dies. When the owner of the capital dies, *mudarabah* is terminated and the *mudarib* has no right to continue with the *mudarabah*. Any further use of the capital depends on the permission of the heirs.

The Differences Between *Musharakah* and *Mudarabah*

Following are the main differences between *musharakah* and *mudarabah* contracts:

- In a partnership (*musharakah*), all partners have to contribute to the capital of partnership, while in a *mudarabah*, only a *sahib al-mal* contribute the capital and a *mudarib* contributes his efforts and expertise.
- In a *musharakah*, all partners can participate in the management of the business, while in a *mudarabah*, the business is run solely by a *mudarib*, and the *sahib al-mal* cannot participate in running the business.
- In a *musharakah*, all partners share the loss to the same ratio in which they invested in the capital of the partnership, while in a *mudarabah*, the loss, if any, is suffered by the *sahib al-mal* only. The *mudarib's* loss is restricted to his labours and efforts. A *mudarib* is only held liable if losses occur due to his negligence or dishonesty.
- Partners in a *musharakah* have unlimited liability. In a case of loss when the asset of *musharakah* is not sufficient to pay for the liabilities of the business, they are transferred to the partners and should be paid by them on a pro rata basis. In contrast, in a *mudarabah* a *sahib al-mal* has a limited liability similar to that of a company's shareholder. His liability is limited to the extent of his investment. The most a *sahib al-mal* may lose is his capital. However, he is not liable if the losses exceed the capital of the *mudarabah* except in cases where a *mudarib* incurred liabilities with the permission of the *sahib al-mal*.[9]
- In a *musharakah*, all the partners jointly own the assets of *musharakah* in proportion to their respective shares in the investment. Each one of them may benefit from the appreciation in the value of the assets. In contrast, in a *mudarabah*, the assets belong solely to the *sahib al-mal*. However, upon liquidation, the asset is sold and the *sahib al-mal* is only entitled to his initial capital.
- There is a disagreement among major schools of *Fiqh* on whether a partner can contribute goods or assets to the capital of *musharakah*. However, all of them agree that the *sahib al-mal* in a *mudarabah* contract should provide cash capital to the *mudarib* and not goods or assets.
- In a *musharakah*, each partner is an agent to each other, while in a *mudarabah*, a *mudarib* is an agent of the *sahib al-mal*, who is the principal, but not vice versa.

Chapter Questions

True/False

1. ( ) A capital provider (*sahib al-mal*) in a *mudarabah* contract may contract *mudarabah* with more than one *mudarib* through a single transaction.
2. ( ) In a *mudarabah* contract, the liability of the capital provider (*sahib al-mal*) is unlimited.

3. ( ) In a *mudarabah,* the owner of the capital may also participate in the management of the business.
4. ( ) In an existing *mudarabah* contract, the *mudarib* does not need the permission of the capital owner to establish a new sub-*mudarabah* contract with others.
5. ( ) In a *mudarabah,* if both partners equally share the profit, they should also equally share the loss.
6. ( ) It is possible for a *mudarib* to claim a fee or a specified wage for his work.
7. ( ) A *sahib al-mal* may provide goods or assets to the *mudarib* as capital of the *mudarabah.*
8. ( ) A *mudarib* can incur debts in the name of *mudarabah* for the purposes of the *mudarabah* business.
9. ( ) In a *mudarabah,* the ownership of the capital provided by the *sahib al-mal* is transferred to the *mudarib.*
10. ( ) A *mudarib* is only held liable if losses occur due to his negligence or dishonesty.

Short Answer

1. In 2009, Zaki agreed to provide RM 200,000 to Ahmad on the basis of a *mudarabah* contract. Zaki did not specify the type of business and left it to Ahmad to decide. Ahmad, who was an IIUM student, thought that there was a good opportunity to invest the money in purchasing cars and leasing them to IIUM students. Ahmad purchased four cars for leasing purposes. Discuss the following:
   a. Who owns the vehicles during the period of the *mudarabah* contract? Do you think that a *mudarib* should jointly own the asset of the *mudarabah* and have a share in the value of the asset when it appreciates or depreciates?
   b. Assuming the parties agree to end the *mudarabah* contract after three years, should Ahmad return to Zaki RM 200,000 or should he return the four vehicles? Please explain how the *sahib al-mal* will redeem his capital.
2. Unlike the Hanafi and Hanbali jurists, the Maliki and Shafi'i jurists do not agree with the imposition of any restrictions on the *mudarib* on the grounds that the *mudarabah* contract is based on trust. Discuss the advantage and disadvantage of imposing restrictions on a *mudarib* in the light of contemporary business environment. Support your arguments with relevant examples.
3. Discuss whether an Islamic bank can use the capital provided by the *sahib al-mal* to enter into another *mudarabah* contract with a *mudarib.*
4. Why can't the provider of the capital (*sahib al-mal*) ask for a guaranteed capital and a guaranteed amount of profit?
5. Who owns the asset that is purchased for the purposes of the business of the *mudarabah*? Support your answer with relevant examples.
6. Compare and contrast the distribution of losses in *mudarabah* and *musharaka* based businesses.
7. Compare and contrast the contract of *murabahah* with interest-based loans.

Notes

1. See Wahbah al-Zuhaili, *Financial Transactions in Islamic Jurisprudence*, vol. 1, trans. Mahmoud A. El-Gamal (Beirut: Dar al-Fikr al-Mouaser, 2003), 493–494.
2. See Ibn Rajib, *Fathul Bari*, vol.4, hadith no. 166.
3. Seeal-Zuhaili, *Financial Transactions in Islamic Jurisprudence*, 513.
4. Ibid. 511.
5. Ibid.
6. See ibid, 507.
7. See ibid, 500–501.
8. See also *The Mejelle*, Article 1423. *The Mejelle*, trans. C.R. Tyser, D. G. Demetriades, Ismail Haqqi Effendi (Petaling Jaya: The Other Press , 2001).
9. See Muhammad Taqi Usmani, "The Concept of Musharakah and Its Application as an Islamic Method of Financing," *Arab Law Quarterly*, vol. 14, no. 3 (2003): 212.

CHAPTER

9

Pledge, Mortgage, or Pawn (*al-Rahn*)

Learning outcomes

At the end of this chapter, you should be able to:

1. Define the pillars and important conditions of the *rahn* contract.
2. Understand the status and position of the pledgor and the pledgee together with their rights and obligations.
3. Explain issues related to the use of the pledged property by the pledgee.

Introduction

Rahn literally means detaining a thing. Legally, *rahn* refers to a contract where a debtor provides a corporeal property to a creditor as a security that enables the creditor to reclaim the debt or to satisfy it out of the pledged property in cases where the debtor is unable or refuses to settle the debt. The Mejjelle defines *rahn* as "to make a property a security in respect of a right of claim, the payment in full of which from that property is permitted."[1] In pledge, the ownership of the pledged property remains with its owner, i.e., the pledgor or the debtor. The pledgee or the creditor is keeping the pledged property as a trust. The concept is presented in Figure 9.1. Pledge (*rahn*) serves as a guarantee, a security, or collateral to the creditor that the debt would be repaid. The concept of *rahn* is mentioned in the *Qur'an*, verse 2: 283 in the context of a debt transaction mentioned in the preceding verse 282. The verse states: "If ye are on a journey, and cannot find a scribe, a pledge with possession (may serve the purpose). And if one of you deposits a thing on trust with another, Let the trustee (Faithfully) discharge His trust, and let him fear his Lord. Conceal not evidence; for whoever conceals it, His heart is tainted with sin. And Allah Knoweth all that ye do."

عَلَى سَفَرٍ وَلَمْ تَجِدُوا كَاتِبًا فَرِهَانٌ مَقْبُوضَةٌ فَإِنْ أَمِنَ بَعْضُكُمْ بَعْضًا فَلْيُؤَدِّ الَّذِي اؤْتُمِنَ أَمَانَتَهُ وَلْيَتَّقِ اللَّهَ رَبَّهُ وَلَا تَكْتُمُوا الشَّهَادَةَ وَمَنْ يَكْتُمْهَا فَإِنَّهُ آثِمٌ قَلْبُهُ وَاللَّهُ بِمَا تَعْمَلُونَ عَلِيمٌ وَإِنْ كُنْتُمْ

In a *hadith* narrated by 'Aishah (mAbpwh), it is reported that "the Prophet (pbAbuh) purchased food grains from a Jew on credit and pledged his iron armor to him."[2]

عائشة قالت: اشترى رسول الله صلى الله عليه وسلم طعاما من يهودي إلى أجل ورهنه درعا له من حديد

FIGURE 9.1 B, the debtor, is called the pledgor, whereas A, the creditor, is called the pledgee. B is the owner of the pledge, whereas A keeps the pledge as collateral.

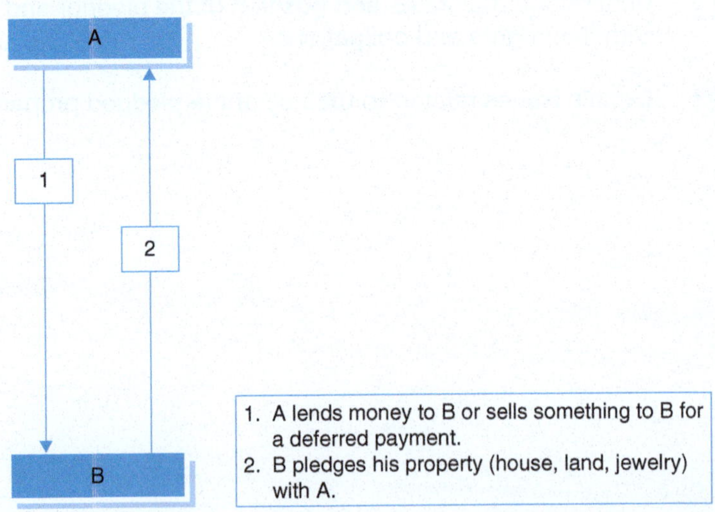

The words in verse 2:283 have led Zahiri scholars to argue that pledge is allowed only in journeys or when it is not possible to get a written agreement or there are no witnesses. The majority of the jurists, however, argue that pledge is allowed both in a journey and when a person is not on a journey. The *hadith* also supports the majority argument. Pledge creates a secure right for the creditor/pledgee, who will be given priority over other creditors. Creditors who have secured their debt through a pledge contract will be given priority over other unsecured creditors in cases of bankruptcy. Pledge also creates a secure right for the first creditor over subsequent creditors with whom the same property is pledged.

Creditors who have secured their debt through a pledge contract will be given priority over other unsecured creditors in cases of bankruptcy.

The Pillars of Pledge (*Rahn*)

According to the majority of *Fiqh* schools, the contract of *rahn* has four pillars. They are:

1. The parties to the contract that are the pledgor (*al-rahin*), who is the debtor and owner of the pledged property, and the pledgee (*al-murtahin*), who is the creditor who takes and keeps the pledged property as a trust.
2. The pledged property (*al-marhun*) is the property that is kept as a security for the debt.
3. The debt (*al-marhunbihi*).
4. Expression that includes offer and acceptance.

Several important conditions exist for *rahn*:

- The parties should have complete legal capacity. They should not suffer from bankruptcy or other obstacles to legal capacity.
- The pledged property should be known and well-defined.
- The pledged property should be capable of coming into the possession of the pledgee. Possession can be both actual (*haqiqii*), as in the case of jewelry, or constructive (*hukmii*), as in the case of land or a house. It is not possible to pledge usufruct, as it is not capable of coming into possession.
- The pledged property should be in existence at the time that the contract of pledge is concluded, and it should be capable of being delivered, because the creditor/pledgee must take its possession. For instance, the pledge of fruits that trees may produce or the pledge of unborn animals is not valid. Similarly, the pledge of agricultural produce that is not yet ripened is not allowed.

- The pledged property should be a valuable (*mutaqawwim*) property. The pledge of prohibited properties or the pledge of properties that cannot be possessed is not valid. Hence, if alcoholic liquor, pork, and such is mortgaged, the transaction will be void.
- A property conjoined with another property cannot be pledged separately. For instance, a house cannot be pledged without the land because possession of a house is not possible without the possession of land, nor can it be sold separately. Similarly, trees without the land cannot be pledged because possession of trees is not possible without the possession of the land.
- The pledged property should be owned by the pledgor, otherwise the contract cannot be executed. However, a guardian or a father may pledge the property of a minor for the debt of a minor or for his own debt.
- The value of the pledged property should be sufficient to cover the amount of debt.

The Use of the Pledge by the Pledgee

The pledge is considered a trust in the hands of the pledgee. He is responsible for its safety and preservation. However, he is liable if the pledged property is damaged or destroyed as a result of his negligence. Pledge is intended to be a security for the payment of debt. It is not meant for investment and profitable use by the pledgee. A *hadith* states, "A pledged property is not forfeited from the owner who has pledged it; he is entitled to its output and is responsible for its expenses."[3]

لا يغلق الرهن من صاحبه الذي رهنه ، له غنمه وعليه غرمه

A pledge contract does not transfer the ownership of the pledge property or its usufruct to the pledgee. Thus, any increase or output of the pledged property belongs to its owner. The Hanafii, Maliki, and Shafi'i jurists agree that the owner/pledgor is entitled to receive the rental payment of house or produce of the land that he has pledged.[4] The pledgee is not allowed to exploit or use the pledged property even with the permission of the pledgor. Exploitation of the pledged property is prohibited based on the principle that "all loans that generate conditional benefit to the lender are usurious." Thus, exploitation and profitable use of the pledge is considered usury. However, if the pledge is an animal that can be used for riding or milk, the pledgee may make use of it in return for the maintenance and feeding of the animal.

Rights and responsibilities of the pledgee:

- The pledgee is entitled to hold the pledged property until he receives a repayment of his debt.
- The pledgee is not entitled to use the pledge, for he has the right to possess it, not to use it. He cannot let or hire the pledge to someone else.
- The pledgee must return the pledge on receiving the payment.

- For a case in which the pledgor refuses to spend on the pledge, the pledgee may do so with the permission of the court and reclaim that from the pledgor.
- The pledgee cannot sell the pledge unless with the consent of the pledgor or a court.
- The pledgee cannot gift or sell the pledged property to another person without the permission of the pledgor/owner.

Rights and responsibilities of the pledgor:

- The pledgor is not allowed to retake his pledge before the settlement of the debt.
- The pledgor cannot reclaim the pledge on the plea of selling it to discharge his debt, except with the consent of the pledgee.
- The pledgor cannot reclaim the pledge on the ground of partial settlement of the debt.
- The pledgor has to pay for the maintenance of the pledge property. This also includes safe-keeping and *takaful* costs.
- Any benefit that accrues from the pledged property belongs to the pledgor who is the owner of the pledge.

A pledge contract does not transfer the ownership of the pledge property or its usufruct to the pledgee.

Forfeiture of the Pledged Property

If the pledgor/debtor is not able to settle his debt, the pledgee/creditor cannot forfeit the pledged property. A hadith states, "A pledged property is not forfeited from the owner who has pledged it; he is entitled to its output and is responsible for its expenses."

لا يغلق الرهن من صاحبه الذي رهنه ، له غنمه وعليه غرمه

If the time for the settlement of debt is fixed, the pledgor/debtor has to settle the debt within that time. If he does not settle the debt, the creditor/pledgee can sell the pledged property and collect his dues, provided that he had been authorised to do so by the pledgor/debtor. If the pledgor refuses to pay and also does not permit the pledgee to sell the pledge, the court may force him either to settle the debt or to allow the sale of the pledge. After the pledge is sold and the debt is settled, the balance, if any, should go to the pledgor. On the other hand, if the price of the pledged property is not enough to satisfy the debt, the pledgor is under an obligation to settle the balance.

If a pledgee dies, his heirs inherit the right to keep the pledged property until the pledgor settles the debt. If a pledgor dies, the contract is dissolved automatically and the debt is payable immediately from the estate of the deceased pledgor.

Chapter Questions

True/False

1. ( ) A person cannot sell his own property if it is pledged with another.
2. ( ) A pledgee has the right to use and benefit from the pledged property since he has provided a loan to the pledgor.
3. ( ) A pledgor who has partially settled the loan cannot reclaim the pledged property.
4. ( ) According to the majority of the *Fiqh* schools, a pledgee can use the pledged property with the permission of the pledgor.
5. ( ) Any profitable use of the pledge property by the pledgee is considered usury.
6. ( ) If a pledgee dies, his heirs inherit the right to keep the pledged property.
7. ( ) If a pledgor cannot settle the loan, the pledged property will automatically belong to the pledgee.
8. ( ) If a pledgor is not able to pay the amount he has borrowed, the pledgee can take the pledged property.
9. ( ) The debt of the pledgor payable at a certain future date should be paid immediately upon his death.
10. ( ) The value of the pledged property could be lower than the amount of debt.

Short Answer

1. Discuss why a pledgee/creditor should not forfeit the pledged property if the pledgor/debtor is not able to settle the debt.
2. State five conditions related to the pledged property that should be fulfilled for concluding a valid pledge contract.
3. Briefly discuss the rights and responsibilities of the pledgor and the pledgee.

Notes

1. See the *Mejelle*, Article 701.
2. Ibn Hajar Fath al-Bari Sharh Sahih al-Bukhari, vol. 5 (Riyad:Bayt al-Afkar al-Dawliyah 1999), 140.
3. See Baihaqi, *Sunan al-Kubra*, vol. 6, 39. See also Imam Malik, al-Muwatta, trans. Aisha Abdurrahman Bewley (Spain: Madinah Press Granad, 1997), 36: 10–14, 300–302.
4. See Wahbah al-Zuhaili, *Financial Transactions in Islamic Jurisprudence*, vol. 2, trans. Mahmoud A. El-Gamal (Beirut: Dar al-Fikr al-Mouaser, 2003), 183–184.

CHAPTER 10

Guarantee (*al-Kafalah*)

Learning outcomes

At the end of this chapter, you should be able to:

1. Define the pillars and conditions of the *kafalah* contract.
2. Understand the types of *kafalah* contracts and their different applications.
3. Explain the rulings related to the charging of a fee for the service of guarantee and its implications.
4. Distinguish a letter of guarantee (LG) issued by banks from the *kafalah* contract.
5. Explain the situations under which a *kafalah* contract would be terminated.

Introduction

Kafalah comes from the root word *kafala,* which means junction, joining, combination, responsibility, or surety. Legally, *kafalah* means the joining of one obligation to another with regard to the settlement of a claim. In *kafalah,* a person joins another in undertaking certain obligation, as shown in Figure 10.1. Consequently, both persons become jointly liable for the settlement of the same obligation. A *hadith* of the Prophet (pbAbuh) is reported to have stated that the surety or a guarantor is liable and the debt should be settled.[1]

الزَّعِيمُ غَارِمٌ وَالدَّيْنُ مَقْضِيٌّ

In another *hadith,* Abu Huraira (mAbpwh) reported that when the body of a dead person having the burden of debt upon him was brought to Allah's Messenger (pbAbuh), he would ask whether he had left property enough to clear off his debt, and if the property left had been sufficient for that (purpose), he observed funeral prayer for him. Otherwise, he said (to his companions), "You observe prayer for your companion. But when Allah opened the gateways of victory for him, he said: I am nearer to the believers than themselves, so if anyone dies leaving a debt, its payment is my responsibility, and if anyone leaves a property, it goes to his heirs."[2]

أَنَّ رَسُولَ اللَّهِ صَلَّى اللَّهُ عَلَيْهِ وَسَلَّمَ كَانَ يُؤْتَى بِالرَّجُلِ الْمَيِّتِ عَلَيْهِ الدَّيْنُ فَيَسْأَلُ هَلْ تَرَكَ لِدَيْنِهِ مِنْ قَضَاءٍ فَإِنْ حُدِّثَ أَنَّهُ تَرَكَ وَفَاءً صَلَّى عَلَيْهِ وَإِلَّا قَالَ صَلُّوا عَلَى صَاحِبِكُمْ فَلَمَّا فَتَحَ اللَّهُ عَلَيْهِ الْفُتُوحَ قَالَ أَنَا أَوْلَى بِالْمُؤْمِنِينَ مِنْ أَنْفُسِهِمْ فَمَنْ تُوُفِّيَ وَعَلَيْهِ دَيْنٌ فَعَلَيَّ قَضَاؤُهُ وَمَنْ تَرَكَ مَالًا فَهُوَ لِوَرَثَتِهِ

FIGURE 10.1 *Kafalah*: Both B and C are jointly liable to settle A's debt.

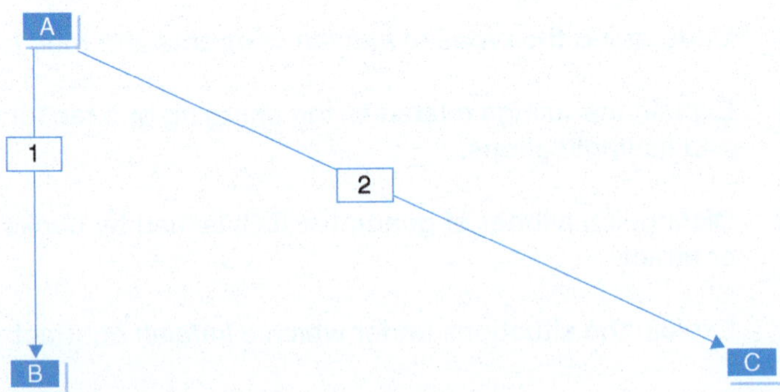

1. A lends money to B or sells something to him for a deferred payment.
2. C agrees to become a guarantor.
3. A can claim his debt from either B or C.

Pillars of *Kafalah*

According to the Hanafii school of *Fiqh*, the contract of *kafalah* has two pillars. They are offer and acceptance. The offer may come from the guarantor and the acceptance from the creditors. According to the majority of the *Fiqh* schools, *kafalah* has four pillars. They are as follows:

1. The guarantor (*kafeel* or *daamin*) who agrees to be jointly liable with the principal debtor for the settlement of his debt.
2. The principal debtor (*makful 'anhu*) or a person in respect of whose default the guarantee is provided.
3. The claim or right that is guaranteed (*makfulbihi*), whether it relates to a person or a debt.
4. The expression, which includes only offer. The majority of the *Fiqh* schools maintain that *kafala* is concluded only by an offer by the guarantor. The acceptance by the creditor is not necessary. Acceptance by the creditor is not required because settlement of his debt does not require his consent.

The Shafi'i jurists have added a creditor (*makfullahu*) to whom the guarantee is provided as a fifth pillar of the *kafalah* contract.

Important conditions for the contract of *kafalah* include:

- The guarantor and the creditor should have complete legal capacity.
- It is not necessary that the principal debtor should have legal capacity. He may be a minor or insane. His presence during the initiation of the guarantee contract is also not necessary. Thus, it is possible to guarantee the debt of an absent person. The consent of the principal debtor is also not necessary.
- The guarantor should give his consent and agree with the guarantee.
- The majority of the Muslim jurists argue that the presence of the creditor during the initiation of the guarantee is not required.
- The guarantor should know the principal debtor. It is not valid to guarantee the debt of an unknown person whose background and current financial ability is not known. This is to enable the guarantor to ascertain whether the principal debtor is able to settle the debt.
- The guarantor should know the creditor. The Hanafii and Shafi'i jurists argue that it is not valid to guarantee the debt of an unknown creditor because repayment of debt is only possible when the creditor is known.
- The claim should be a debt and should not arise from a trust (*amanah*). Trust-based claims are not considered debts and cannot be guaranteed. For example, a depository, a partner, a *mudarib*, a lessee, or a pledgee are trustees. They hold the properties on trust and are not liable for any loss unless negligence on their part is proven. Hence, they are not guarantor for the properties they hold on trust. They also could not be required to provide a guarantor.
- The claim should be known in terms of quantity, quality, and type. *Kafalah* is not allowed when the parties are ignorant about the claim.

The Effects of *Kafalah*

Once a valid *kafalah* is concluded, it establishes a right to the creditor to claim the debt either from the principal debtor or the guarantor, as shown in Figure 10.1. The principal debtor is not released from the debt. Imam Malik, in one of his opinions, says that the creditor should not claim the debt from the guarantor unless the principal debtor is unable to pay. The majority of the Muslim jurists, however, say that the creditor has an option whether to demand the payment of debt either from the principal debtor or from the guarantor. When a guarantor pays the debt to the creditor, he has a right to claim it from the principal debtor.

When a guarantor pays the debt to the creditor, he has a right to claim it from the principal debtor.

Immediate, Conditional, and Suspended *Kafalah*

Kafalah can be immediate, conditional, and contingent. In an immediate *kafalah,* the guarantee takes effect upon a person agreeing to become a guarantor. For example, a person may agree to unconditionally become a guarantor for a debt. In this case, the guarantee will follow the debt. If the debt has to be paid immediately, the guarantor is liable to pay it immediately. If the debt is deferred or payable by instalments in a certain period, the guarantor is liable to settle the debt accordingly. Any variation to the date of settlement or mode of payment has to be agreed upon by the creditor. A guarantee could also be conditional when a person becomes a guarantor if certain conditions are met. In such a case, the guarantee takes effect when the conditions are met. For instance, a person may stipulate to become a guarantor if a debtor leaves a certain city or country. In such a case, the guarantee takes effect when the principal debtor leaves the city or the country. *Kafalah* can also be contingent or deferred to a future date where the provision of guarantee would depend on the happening of a certain incident. For instance, a person may stipulate to become a guarantor if another lends a certain known amount to a specified person. According to Imam Abu Hanifah and some Hanbali jurists, the provision of *kafalah* may also depend on the arrival of a certain specified time. For instance, the provision of a guarantee may depend on the arrival of next month or year. However, the Shafi'i jurists do not agree with the time-based *kafalah.*[3]

Types of *Kafalah*

The claim that is guaranteed could be in relation to a person, the settlement of a debt, the return of a thing, or the performance of an act or service. Based on this, the contract of *kafalah* could generally be divided into two types: *kafalah* for a person (*kafalah bin-nafs*) and *kafalah* for a property (*kafalahbil-mal*). In a guarantee for a person, the guarantor is assuming the responsibility to make sure that the principal (defendant), in a civil lawsuit, will be present or appear at a specified date. For instance, a guarantor may only guarantee the presence and appearance of the principal debtor at a court on a specified date. In this case, he is not guaranteeing to the creditor the settlement of his debt but the mere appearance of the principal debtor. The guarantor is, in this case, required only to make sure of the presence of the principal debtor whenever he or she is needed. The guarantor is not liable to settle the debt on behalf of the principal debtor. If the principal debtor dies, the guarantor is not bound to pay for his or her debt. This is because the guarantee given is only for the presence of the principal and not for the settlement of his debt. The jurists agree that guaranteeing the appearance or the presence of an accused in a criminal case, such as murder or theft, is not valid, because the criminal, whose appearance and presence is guaranteed, may not be traced and it is not possible to punish a guarantor for a crime not committed by him or her.

Kafalah for a property can be a guarantee for the settlement of a debt (*dayn*) or a guarantee that a certain specific sold item (*'ain*) would be delivered or a specific act would be performed. In such cases, the creditor has the right to claim the debt either from the principal debtor or the guarantor. Similarly, the purchaser can demand the delivery of the sold item, either from the seller or the guarantor. A guarantor is not freed of liability if the principal debtor dies. The creditor or the purchaser of the item can demand that the guarantor settle the debt or deliver the item.

Charging a Fee for the Service of Guarantee

Can a guarantor ask a principal debtor for a fee for rendering the service of guarantee? A creditor is prohibited to charge the debtor an additional amount, as this is usury. Similarly, a guarantor who does not provide any debt is also prohibited to charge the debtor. If a guarantor charges a fee for his service, the principal debtor will have to pay the amount of debt to the creditor and a fee to the guarantor. The debtor would have to pay more than the amount of debt. Thus, the creditor is not allowed to charge interest and the guarantor cannot ask for a fee. The debtor is protected against both. *Kafalah,* therefore, is a gratuitous contract, and the service rendered by a guarantor is done freely without charging any fees.

Can a guarantor charge a creditor a premium for providing him a guarantee that the debt would be settled? The provision of *kafalah* should be for a genuine reason for which a guarantor, after examining the financial status of the debtor, would guarantee the settlement of his debt. However, if a guarantee is provided for a fee, it will transform the gratuitous *kafalah* into a business for profiteering purposes. *Kafalah* is different from insurance. An insurance company would provide compensation to affected policyholders for cases in which certain specified incidents happen. The affected ones could be few in number and most probably are qualified to claim compensation for genuine reasons. However, if insurance is provided to creditors, they will be willing to pay a premium to an insurance company who would guarantee the settlement of their debts. Subsequently, it will encourage the creation and proliferation of more debts and subprime debts. This is particularly harmful in an atmosphere in which creditors can sell their debts to third parties. Moreover, there is always the possibility of mass default triggered by sharp increases of prices, unemployment, or other factors. The aggregate outcome of such practices could be catastrophic to the financial system, as was seen during the 2007–2008 financial and economic crises. Thus, the practice of charging a fee for the service of guarantee runs contrary to the public interest. In contrast, when a guarantee is provided without monetary or pecuniary expectations, it will be more genuine and protect the interest of both the creditor and the guarantor. Thus, guaranteeing should not be turned into a business that would generate revenue for the guarantor.

If a guarantee is provided for a fee, it will transform the gratuitous kafalah *into a business for profiteering purposes.*

Letter of Guarantee

In international trade, the payment of the price cannot be simultaneous with the supply of the goods. The sellers/exporters and the purchasers/importers may not know each other or they cannot trust each other. There has to be an intermediary who can guarantee the payment of price. The bank comes in to fill in the gap and provide the guarantee service. The bank, therefore, can charge a fee for providing the service. When a bank issues a letter of guarantee (LG) based on *kafalah*, the bank first requires the customer to deposit the amount for which the LG is sought from the bank. An LG is next issued based on the amount that is deposited with the bank. This act of the debtor depositing with the bank distinguishes it from the *kafalah* contract because, in a *kafalah* contract, the guarantor does not ask the principal debtor to deposit the amount with him. Thus, the practice is not similar with the *kafalah* contract. When a bank issues LG to a customer, it is issued on the certainty that the customer has already deposited the money with the bank. Because this is not exactly what a *kafalah* contract is, the charging of fees by the bank can be justified. The bank can charge for the service of issuing an LG to a purchaser who is willing to pay the price but has no means to directly pay to the seller. Because it is not a *kafalah* contract, an Islamic bank can charge a fee for the service it renders based on the contract of *ja'aalah* or based on the concept of freedom of contract because it is an act that is not prohibited. It is also possible to argue that an LG is an example of a depository who would become a guarantor for the debt of a depositor. The arrangement may also fall under *hawalah.*

Termination of *Kafalah*

A contract of *kafalah* may come to an end in the following situations:

- When the principal debtor or the guarantor settles the debt or when the creditor makes the debt a gift, either to the principal debtor or to the guarantor.

- When a creditor releases the principal debtor from the debt, the guarantor is also released. However, if a creditor releases the guarantor from the claim through arbitration, either partially or fully, the principal debtor is not released. The creditor can claim the balance from the principal debtor.
- When the debt is transferred through *hawalah* to a third party, both the principal debtor and the guarantor are released.
- The death of the guarantor for the property does not terminate the contract of *kafalah*. If the guarantor for the property dies, the obligation of guarantee does not cease because it could be discharged by means of the estate that the guarantor has left. On the other hand, the death of the principal debtor or the guarantor in a contract of *kafala* for the person terminates the contract.
- The creditor can terminate the contract of *kafalah* even if the principal debtor or the guarantor does not agree.

Chapter Questions

True/False

1. ( ) According to the majority of *Fiqh* schools, in a contract of guarantee (*kafalah*), the creditor can demand the settlement of debt either from the principal debtor or the guarantor.
2. ( ) If a guarantor guarantees the payment of debt, the creditor cannot claim the debt from the principal debtor.
3. ( ) In a contract of guarantee (*kafalah*), a guarantor who settles the debt can claim the amount from the principal debtor.
4. ( ) In a contract of guarantee (*kafalah*), if a creditor releases the principal debtor from the obligation, then the guarantor (*kafeel*) is also released.
5. ( ) In a contract of guarantee (*kafalah*), it is not necessary for the principal debtor to have complete legal capacity.
6. ( ) In a contract of *kafalah*, if the principal debtor is released from the liability, the guarantor is not released.
7. ( ) The creditor can dissolve the contract of guarantee (*kafalah*), even if the principal debtor does not agree.
8. ( ) The creditor can only terminate the guarantee (*kafalah*) contract with the consent of the principal debtor and the guarantor.
9. ( ) When a creditor cancels the guarantee contract, the principal debtor is still liable to settle the debt.
10. ( ) In a contract of guarantee (*kafalah*), a guarantor who cannot settle the debt should withdraw from the guarantee contract.

Short Answer

1. Discuss the division of *kafalah* into *kafalah* for the person and *kafalah* for the property.
2. Can a guarantor charge the principal debtor a fee for the service of guarantee he or she provides?
3. Can a guarantor charge the creditor a fee for the service of guarantee he or she provides?
4. What are the claims for which a guarantee could not be provided?
5. Can a guarantor who settles the debt claim the amount from the principal debtor?

Notes

1. Al-Hafiz Abi Abdullah ibn Yazid Al-Qazwini, *Sunan Ibn Majah* (Beirut: Dar al-Fikir, 2003), vol. 7, p. 240. Hadith no. 2396.
2. Muslim ibn al-Hajjaj al-Qushayri, *Sahih Muslim* (Beirut: Dar Ihya' al-Turath al-'Arabi, 2000), vol. 8, p. 351, Hadith no. 3040.
3. See as-Sayyid Sabiq, *Fiqhu as-Sunnah* (Cairo: Dar al-Hadith, 2004), 1010–1011.

CHAPTER 11

Transfer of Debt (*al-Hawalah*)

Learning outcomes

At the end of this chapter, you should be able to:

1. Define the pillars, important conditions, and effects of a *hawalah* contract.
2. Discuss the juristic rulings concerning the status and types of *hawalah* contract.
3. Compare and contrast the contract of *hawalah* with the contracts of *suftajah*, *kafalah,* and *bay' al-dayn.*
4. Explain the situations under which a *hawalah* contract would be terminated.

Introduction

Literally, *hawalah* means transfer or change. Legally, *hawalah* is defined as a contract through which the liability for the settlement of a debt is transferred from a principal debtor (*muheel*) to a transferee (*muhalalaihi*). The model is presented in Figure 11.1. According to the majority of the *Fiqh* schools, the transferee (*muhalalaihi*) to whom the debt is transferred must be indebted to the principal debtor (*muheel*). The Hanafii jurists argue that the transfer of debt may or may not be linked to the debt that the transferee may or may not owe the principal debtor.

Hawalah abolishes the existing debt between the creditor and the principal debtor and between the principal debtor and the transferee, and it establishes a new debt between the creditor and the transferee. Hence, *hawalah* cancels two debts and creates a new one. *Hawalah* is similar to the sale of debt, but it is not sale; it also resembles *kafalah* and *wakalah*. However, it is a unique contract that has its own distinct features and conditions. The three important participants in a *hawalah* contract are the creditor, the principal debtor, and the transferee. When a valid *hawalah* is concluded, the debt is no longer demanded from the principal debtor. The three effects of a *hawalah* contract are the transfer of a debt and the liability for its payment from the principal debtor to the transferee, the release of the principal debtor from debt and liability, and the resulting right of the creditor to claim the debt from the transferee. As such, the principal debtor is released from the liability, and the creditor can only demand the settlement of his debt from the transferee.

Hawalah *abolishes the existing debt between the creditor and the principal debtor and between the principal debtor and the transferee, and it establishes a new debt between the creditor and the transferee.*

FIGURE 11.1 **B owes A a debt and C owes B a debt. The parties agree to enter into a *hawalah* contract. B's obligation to A is transferred to C. Consequently B is released from debt and A can claim the debt from C.**

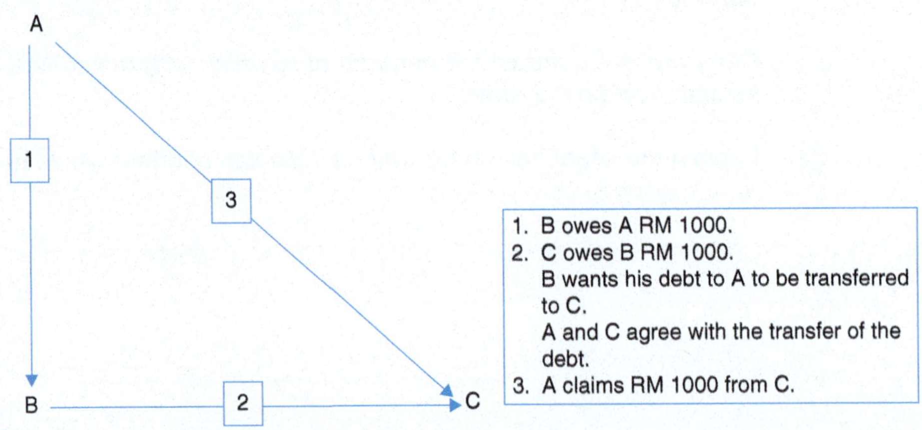

Abu Huraira (mAbpwh) reported that Allah's Messenger (pbAbuh) has stated, "Procrastination in paying debts by a wealthy man is injustice. So, if your debt is transferred from your debtor to a trustworthy rich debtor you should agree."[1]

عَنْ أَبِي هُرَيْرَةَأَنَّ رَسُولَ اللَّهِ صَلَّى اللَّهُ عَلَيْهِ وَسَلَّمَ قَالَ مَطْلُ الْغَنِيِّ ظُلْمٌ وَإِذَا أُتْبِعَ أَحَدُكُمْ عَلَى مَلِيءٍ فَلْيَتْبَعْ

According to the Hanbali and Zahiri jurists, the *hadith* conveys a binding command, and, as such, it creates an obligation (*wajib*). Consequently, they argue that, for a valid *hawalah* the consent of the principal debtor is required. Once the principal debtor initiates the *hawalah,* and the creditor and the transferee are informed, they are bound to accept the transfer of debt and should agree with it as the *hadith* indicates. The Hanbali jurists contend that the transferee is under obligation to settle the debt that he owes to the principal debtor. According to them, it does not matter whether the principal debtor personally claims his debt from the transferee or he empowers another to claim it. This, they say, is similar to a situation in which an agent collects the debts on behalf of his principal. These scholars, therefore, argue that it is not necessary that the transferee should give his consent.

According to the majority of the *Fiqh* schools, the *hadith* only conveys a recommendation (*istihbab*). The Maliki and Shafi'i jurists argue that the consent of the principal debtor and the creditor is required for a valid *hawalah.* They argue that the principal debtor has the options to decide how he should settle his debt and should not be forced to settle it in any given way. They also argue that since the creditor owns the debt, his consent is required for any transfer of that debt to another person whose creditworthiness and promptness in settlement of debts could be different from the principal debtor. In contrast, they argue that the consent of the transferee is not required, and he is obliged to agree with the transfer of debt, because the transferee owes a debt to the principal debtor. The principal debtor may him- or herself collect the debt or authorise another to collect his or her debt from the transferee.

The Hanafii jurists also agree that the *hadith* only conveys a recommendation (*istihbab*). They argue that, for a valid *hawalah,* the consent of the principal debtor, the creditor, and the transferee is required. The consent of the principal debtor is needed because he has to initiate the process. Similarly, they argue that the creditor owns the debt, and it cannot be transferred except with his or her consent. Moreover, debtors differ in their creditworthiness and promptness in settlement of their debts. As such, they argue, the consent of the creditor is also required. They also argue that, by transferring the debt to the transferee, *hawalah* amounts to appropriating the property, and this should not be done except with the transferee's consent. The fact that the transferee owes a debt to the principal debtor does not change the situation because people differ in their degree of aggressiveness when collecting their debts. Therefore, they argue, there is no obligation on the transferee unless he accepts the *hawalah.* They further argue that the consent of the creditor is also required. This is due to the fact that people differ in their abilities to settle their debts. The transferee may not be able to pay the creditor or he may settle the debt in a longer period.[2]

Pillars of *Hawalah*

According to the Hanafii jurists, the contract of *hawalah* has two pillars. They are offer from the principal debtor and acceptance from the creditor and the transferee. The majority of the *Fiqh* schools say that *hawalah* has six pillars. They are: the principal debtor, the creditor, the transferee, the debt that the principal debtor owes to the creditor, the debt owed by the transferee to the principal debtor, and the expression, which includes offer and acceptance.

Important conditions of *hawalah*:

- All three parties should have complete legal capacity.
- The parties should consent and agree with the transfer of debt (*hawalah*) contract. In this regard, see the rulings of various jurists as discussed earlier.
- The acceptance of the creditor and the transferee should be given during the session of the contract.
- The subject matter of *hawalah* should be debt (*dayn*) and not a specific thing (*'ain*). For instance, a book borrowed is considered a specific thing and cannot become the subject matter of a *hawalah* contract.
- Both the debts, that is, the debt that the principal debtor owes the creditor and the debt that the transferee owes the principal debtor, should be known.
- Both the debts should be equal in kind and amount. It is not allowed if one of them is more or less than the other. Otherwise, the contract will not be *hawalah* but falls within the forbidden sale contract in which a debt is traded for another. Similarly, *hawalah* is not valid if the principal debt is mature and the debt on the transferee is payable at a fixed future time.
- The debts or one of them should not arise from a *salam* contract because the parties cannot deal with the *salam* commodity unless they obtain its possession.
- The transferor (*muhil*) should owe a debt to the transferred party (*muhal*). In the absence of such a debt, if the transferred party (*muhal*) is referred to the transferee, the contract is not a transfer of debt (*hawalah*), but agency (*wakalah*). In this case, the transferred party (*muhal*) is collecting the debt on behalf of the transferor (*muhil*).
- According to the majority of the *Fiqh* schools, the transferee should owe a debt to the principal debtor. If the transferee is not indebted to the principal debtor and agrees to pay the creditor, the contract is changed to *kafalah*. In this case, the transferee is paying for the principal debtor. Consequently, all the conditions of a valid *kafalah* are applicable. The Hanafii jurists, on the other hand, argue that it is not required that that the principal debtor should owe the transferee. The transferee, for instance, could be a depositor or could, for any other reason, agree with the transfer of debt.

Types of *Hawalah*

According to the Hanafii jurists, there are two types of *hawalah*. They are restricted and unrestricted *hawalah*.

1. Unrestricted transfer of debt (*hawalahmutlaqah*) is a type of *hawalah* in which a principal debtor transfers the debt to a transferee without linking the transfer to a debt that the transferee may or may not owe the principal debtor and the transferee accepts the transfer of debt (*hawalah*). For instance, a principal debtor may use the language of *hawalah* to transfer the debt to a person with whom he has deposited his money without linking the transfer to the deposited money. If the depository accepts the transfer of debt, the *hawalah* contract is concluded. The principal debtor is released from the debt, and the creditor can demand the payment of debt only from the transferee, that is, the depository. In this case the depositor may also claim his deposit from the depository. Consequently, the depository becomes liable for two claims.

   According to the majority of the *Fiqh* schools, a valid transfer of debt should be linked to the debt that the transferee owes the principal debtor. This debt according to them is one of the pillars of *hawalah,* and its nonexistence means that there is no *hawalah* contract. They argue that if a debt is transferred, without linking it with the debt that the transferee owes the principal debtor, or if such a debt does not exist at all and the transferee agrees to settle the debt, such arrangement falls under *kafalah* and not *hawalah.* Accordingly, the transferee in such cases, they argue, is a guarantor, and the principal debtor is not released from the liability. The creditor can claim the debt either from the principal debtor or the guarantor.
2. Restricted transfer of debt (*hawalahmuqayyidah*) is a type of *hawalah* in which a principal debtor transfers his debt to a transferee who owes him a debt. The majority of the *Fiqh* schools only recognise this type of transfer of debt as a *hawalah.*

Transfer of Right (*Hawalat al-Haqq*)

Hawalat al-Haqq refers to the transfer of right from one creditor to another. Although, in transfer of debt, one debtor replaces another, in transfer of right, one creditor replaces another. For instance, a seller may refer a purchaser to pay the price of the sold item to his (the seller's) creditor. It may also happen when a pledgee/creditor wants the pledgor to pay the debt to his (the pledgee's) creditor. In transfer of right (*hawalatal-haq*), the creditor takes the initiative, whereas in transfer of debt (*hawalat al-dayn*), the debtor takes the initiative.

Bill of Exchange (*Suftaja*)

Muslim jurists used the term *Suftajah* to describe a loan contract in which a creditor stipulates another place for the settlement of the loan. A creditor, by stipulating another place, city, or country for the settlement of the loan, can benefit in two ways. First, the creditor wants to transfer the fund from one place to another without taking the risk of insecurity that is usually associated with the transfer of a large sum of money. Second, the creditor wants to avoid the payment of fees that he or she otherwise would have to pay for the transfer of money from one place to another.

The Shafi'is and Malikis have prohibited any condition that can benefit the creditor in any of these two ways. According to them, any condition stipulating the settlement of loan in a place other than the one in which the loan is given benefits the creditor and is prohibited.[3] The Hanbalis argue that a lender may benefit from the loan contract provided this does not harm the borrower. Accordingly, they argue that it is valid to stipulate the settlement of loan in another place provided it does not cause any inconvenience to the debtor and there is no risk of insecurity.[4] They did not prohibit it if it did not result in any harm to the borrower. According to the Hanafiis, *suftajah* is strongly disliked to the extent of prohibition (*karahahtahreemi*).[5]

Termination of *Hawalah*

The contract of *hawalah* would be terminated in the following situations:

- If *hawalah* is cancelled (*faskh*) before it becomes effective or executed, then the creditor has the right to make a claim against the principal debtor.
- The Hanafii jurists argue that there must be recourse to the principal debtor for cases in which the transferee becomes bankrupt or dies bankrupt, or he denies having consented to the transfer and the creditor has no evidence against him. They argue that *hawalah* is intended to secure the right of the creditor and, because it is impossible to collect the debt from the transferee, the contract, therefore, is terminated and the debt is retransferred to the principal debtor (transferor). The majority of the *Fiqh* schools argue that a valid *hawalah* contract transfers the debt to the transferee. The debt according to them should never be retransferred to the principal debtor even if the transferee is dead or bankrupt. According to them, the creditor before giving his consent to the transfer of debt should have investigated whether the transferee is bankrupt or not. In this case, his position is similar to a person who has bought a certain property for a price higher than the market price. However, the Malikii and the Hanbali jurists argue that, if the creditor has stipulated that the transferee should not be in financial constraints or bankrupt, and later it is found that the transferee is bankrupt, then he can claim his debt from the principal debtor. The Malikii jurists also say that the debt can be retransferred to the principal debtor if he has cheated the creditor and transfers the debt to a person who is bankrupt.
- The *hawalah* comes to an end when the transferee pays the debt to the creditor.
- If the creditor gives the debt as a gift to the transferee and the latter accepts it.
- If the creditor makes the debt as a charity (*sadaqah*) to the transferee.
- If the creditor releases the transferee from the debt (*ibra*).

The Differences Between *Hawalah* and *Kafalah*

Following are the differences between *hawalah* and *kafalah* contracts:

- In hawalah the principal debtor is released from the debt, whereas in *kafalah* he is not.
- In *hawalah*, the creditor can claim the debt only from the transferee, whereas in *kafalah*, the creditor can claim the debt either from the principal debtor or the guarantor.

- In *hawalah,* according to the majority of the *Fiqh* schools, the transferee should owe the principal debtor, whereas in *kafalah* the guarantor does not owe any debt to the principal debtor.
- *Kafalah* can refer to a person's debt or to a thing or with regard to the availability of a person, whereas *hawalah* can only refer to a debt.
- Guarantee (*kafalah*) is required at the initial stage when a debt is created, whereas *hawalah* could be resorted to at a later stage when the debt is transferred.
- *Kafalah* only needs an offer by a guarantor to be concluded, whereas *hawalah* needs the consent of all the parties.
- In *hawalah,* the transferee has to oblige and accept the transfer of debt, whereas in a *kafalah* contract, a person voluntarily becomes a guarantor.
- A guarantor provides a gratuitous service, whereas the transferee does not provide such a service because he is already indebted to the principal debtor.

The Difference Between *Hawalah* and the Sale of Debt (*Bay' al-Dayn*)

Following are the differences between the contracts of *hawalah* and *bay' al-dayn:*

- In *hawalah* a debt is transferred for its par value, whereas in *bay' al-dayn,* it is sold for a discount.
- In *hawalah,* according to the majority of the *Fiqh* schools, the transferee owes the principal debtor, whereas in *bay' al-dayn,* the purchaser of the debt does not owe the debtor.
- In *hawalah,* it is the principal debtor who transfers the debt, whereas in *bay' al-dayn,* it is the creditor who sells it.
- *Hawalah* is a permissible contract, whereas the validity of *bay' al-dayn* is disputed by Muslim jurists.
- In *hawalah,* in certain cases, there could be recourse to the principal debtor if the transferee does not pay the debt. In contrast, in *bay al-dayn,* there is no recourse to the creditor if the debtor does not pay.

Chapter Questions

True/False

1. ( ) In a transfer of debt (*hawalah*) contract, the debt is transferred for a higher price.
2. ( ) In a transfer of debt (*hawalah*) contract, the debt is transferred for a discount.
3. ( ) The majority of the *Fiqh* schools argue that, if a transferee does not owe any debt to the principal debtor, the arrangement falls under the guarantee (*kafalah*) contract.

4. ( ) In a contract of *hawalah,* the creditor can claim the debt either from the principal debtor or from the transferee.
5. ( ) In a *suftajah,* a person provides a loan to another on the condition that the latter should settle the loan in a different place.
6. ( ) According to the majority of the Muslim jurists, a valid transfer of debt should not be linked to the debt that the transferee owes the principal debtor.
7. ( ) The subject matter of a *hawalah* contract could also be a specific thing such as a book.
8. ( ) When a *hawalah* contract is concluded, the two existing debts are cancelled and a new debt is created.
9. ( ) According to the Hanafii jurists, in certain situations in a *hawalah* contract a creditor may have recourse to the principal debtor.
10. ( ) A *hawalah* contract comes to an end when the transferee settles the debt.

Short Answer

1. When is it possible for a borrower to transfer (*hawalah*) the debt to another person? State what the pillars of a *hawalah* contract are.
2. State the main differences between *hawalah* and *bay' al-dayn* contracts.
3. State the main differences between *kafalah* and *hawalah* contracts.

Notes

1. Sahih Muslim, vol. 8, 205, Hadith no. 2924.
2. See Wahbah al-Zuhaili, *Financial Transactions in Islamic Jurisprudence,* vol. 2, trans. Mahmoud A. El-Gamal (Beirut: Dar al-Fikr al-Mouaser, 2003), 52–54.
3. Al-Dasuqi, *Hashiyat al-Dasuqi,* vol. 3, 225–226. See also Al-Shirazi, Abu Ishaq Ibrahim ibn 'Ali, *Al-Muhadhdhab,* vol. 1 (Beirut: Dar al-Kutub al-'Imiyyah, 1995), 304.
4. Ibn Qudamah, *Al-Mughni,* vol. 4 (Qairo: Dar al-Hadith, 2004), 390–391.
5. Ibn 'Abidin, *Hashiyat,* vol. 4 (Makkah al-Mukarramah: Maktabat Makkah al-Mukarramah, 1986), 295.

CHAPTER 12

The Contracts of Absolution (*al-Ibra*) and Set-Off (*al-Muqassah*)

Learning outcomes

At the end of this chapter, you should be able to:

1. Define the pillars and conditions of *ibra.*
2. Understand the effects, types, and applications of *ibra.*
3. Explain issues related to the conditional *ibra* and the various juristic discussions on its validity.
4. Distinguish between the contracts of *ibra* and *hibah.*
5. Define the pillars and conditions of *muqassah.*
6. Understand the effects, types, and applications of *muqassah.*

Introduction

Ibra' literally means "release, removal, relief, or abandoning." Legally, *absolution (ibra)* refers to a contract through which a person waives or drops a right that is established as a liability on another. For example, *ibra* is concluded when a creditor releases his debtor from the payment of debt. *Ibra* is a charitable gratuitous contract. It is a recommended (*mandub*) act, and the provider of *ibra* is rewarded. The *Qur'an* states, "If, however, (the debtor) is in strained circumstance, (grant him) a delay until a time of ease, and it would be for your own good—if you knew it—to remit (the debt entirely) by way of charity" (2:280).

وإن كان ذو عسرة فنظرة إلى ميسرة، وأن تصدقوا خير لكم ان كنتم تعلمون

Absolution (*ibra*) implies both the dropping of a right and its transfer to another person. In the latter sense, *ibra* implies the transfer of ownership over a right. This has given *ibra* a dual character. For instance, when a debtor is released, the debt is dropped. However, from another perspective it is also possible to argue that the ownership over the debt is transferred to the debtor. The Hanafii and the majority of Hanbali and some Shafi'i jurists argue that the dominant aspect of *ibra* is the dropping or annulment (*isqaat*) of a right. The Hanafii jurists also argue that once a debt is dropped it cannot be reinstated. The majority of the Maliki jurists argue that the dominant aspect of *ibra* is the transfer of ownership. Accordingly, any offer of *ibra* needs to be accepted by the recipient.[1]

Absolution (ibra) *implies both the dropping of a right and its transfer to another person.*

The Subject Matter of *Ibra*

The proper subject matters of *ibra* are debt (*dayn*), right (*haqq*), and claims over a nonfungible property or a thing (*'ain*). Debts are the most common subject matter of *ibra* in situations in which a creditor drops his debt and releases the debtor. Accordingly, debts of fungible properties, such as rice, sugar, or money, can be dropped or annulled as they are considered as an obligation (*dayn*) that could be established as a liability.

Ibra can also be exercised in relation to rights that concern humans. For instance, a creditor may release a guarantor in a contract of *kafalah*, or a creditor may release a transferee in a contract of *hawalah*. Similarly, a person may waive his right to use a certain property, or his right to cancel a contract based on the option of defect, or his right to claim compensation for the destruction of his property. *Ibra* is not valid with regard to the rights of Allah (swt) (*huqullah*). For instance, the punishment for a perpetrator of rape, false accusation, or theft cannot be waived after the matter has reached the court and a judge convicts him. However, *ibra* can be made by the heirs of a murder victim with regard to the right of retribution for killing or murder.

Borrowing of nonfungible properties such as a book or a computer is not considered a debt (*dayn*) and cannot be dropped. The book or the computer will remain in the ownership of the lender. In such cases, a mere drop of right in favour of the borrower of the book or computer is not enough, but a clear transfer of ownership through other contracts such as a gift or sale is needed. However, other claims regarding a nonfungible property (*'ain*) could also become the subject matter of *ibra*. These may include, for instance, the right to demand the return of a certain thing, such as a book or a car, or the delivery of a sold item. In such cases, the rights could be dropped, but the ownership over those items remains with the owner. In contrast to debt (*dayn*), which can be dropped by an *ibra*, it is not possible to use *ibra* in relation to a thing itself (*'ain*) because it amounts to the dropping or cancellation of ownership right over that thing, which is not accepted by all *Fiqh* schools.

The Pillars of *Ibra*

The Hanafii jurists argue that the contract of *ibra* has only one pillar of offer because they view ibra as a dropping of a right. According to the majority of the jurists, *ibra* has four pillars. They are:

1. The creditor or a person who has dropped his right.
2. The debtor or a person who is absolved from an obligation.
3. The claim, right, or debt that is dropped.
4. The offer and acceptance.

The majority of the jurists view *ibra* in substance as the dropping of a creditor's right. They argue that *ibra* becomes effective when a person declares the dropping of his or her right or cancels his or her debt. They say that acceptance by the debtor is not required. For instance, a creditor may say to a debtor, "I release you from the debt, or I have no claim on you, or I have no right on you, or you have settled the debt fully." In these situations the debtor does not need to accept the offer. The Maliki jurists, on the other hand, view *ibra* as a transfer of ownership of a debt to the debtor. They argue that *ibra* is similar to a gift and it therefore requires acceptance on the part of the debtor. The Shafi'is and Hanbalis are of the opinion that *ibra'* is valid even if rejected by the debtor. The Hanafiis and Malikis, on the other hand, think that *ibra'* is not valid when rejected. The Hanafiis argue that although *ibra* does not require acceptance, it is invalid if rejected. Thus, if a creditor releases the debtor from the debt, *ibra* is still valid, even if there is no acceptance from the debtor. However, in case of rejection by the debtor, *ibra* has no effect. Hence, if one person releases another from debt, there is no condition that the person released should accept it. However, if he does not accept it, the *ibra* has no effect.[2]

Important conditions for *ibra*:

- The creditor should have complete legal capacity. *Ibra* is not valid from a prodigal or a bankrupt person.
- The creditor should be the owner of the right or an agent acting on behalf of the owner.

- The creditor should give his consent; if consent is forced, it is not valid.
- The debtor should be known and specified.
- According to the Shafi'is, the claim or debt should be made known because consent cannot be given for a claim that is not known unless it is done through *wasiyyah*. For instance, it is not valid if a creditor says that he has released his debtor from one of the two debts or when the amount is not known. The majority of the Muslim jurists, however, do not stipulate this. For example, I have released you from one of the two debts or when the amount of debt is not known.
- The claim should not be a thing (*'ain*)because it cannot be established on the *dhimmah*. It is valid only with respect to a debt (*dayn*) and right (*haqq*)—for instance, when a creditor releases a guarantor from the guarantee in a *kafalah* contract or when a creditor releases a transferee from the claim in a *hawalah* contract.
- The claim should be in existence when *ibra* is made. *Ibra* is not valid with regard to claims that may come into existence in the future. For example, a person cannot release another from a debt that has not occurred yet. Release of a debt or a liability prior to its existence is not valid. Similarly, a right prior to its existence cannot be waived. Similarly, the heirs cannot make *ibra* in favour of each other while the person from whom they inherit is still alive. The right should already be in existence. In other words, the expression should be made in relation to an already established right and not in relation to a future right. For instance, it is not valid when a person is released from paying the price for a thing that he will buy tomorrow or a woman releases her future husband from the payment of alimony (*mahr*) or the obligation of maintenance.
- The majority of the Muslim jurists stipulate that an offer of *ibra* should be immediate, should not depend on a condition, and should not be suspended in the future. However, an offer of *ibra* may depend on the condition of payment of the balance. For instance, a creditor may tell the debtor, "I have released you from 50 percent or 30 percent of the debt on the condition that you pay me the balance." It is valid according to the Hanafis, Malikis, and Shafi'is, as this is receiving some of the debt and forgiving the balance. The Hanabalis, however, say it is not valid.
- The Malikis, however, allow suspension of *ibra* to a future date. According to them, it is valid if an offer of *ibra* is suspended until the payment of the balance. For instance, a creditor may say to his debtor: "You are released from half the debt when you pay the other half." However, if a person makes the offer of *ibra* dependent on death, it is valid because it becomes *wasiyyah*.
- It is also not permitted for a creditor to release the debtor from some of the debt on the condition that the latter should accelerate or bring forward the payment of the balance or pay the balance in a shorter period, because this may resemble usury. However, if a debtor pays some of the debt in advance of the appointed date, without any condition, the creditor may take from him and release him from the balance.
- *Ibra* should not go against the rules of *Shari'ah*. For instance, in a currency exchange (*sarf*) contract, a person cannot release another from the condition of possession of currencies.

Similarly, it is not possible for a person to release him- or herself from the duty of guardianship over a minor. This is because *ibra* must not lead to the violation of another person's right, such as a mother annulling her right of custody over a child in favour of another person. It may amount to injustice to the child and violates his/her right. The right of custody over a minor child is given to the mother. Thus, in these cases, *ibra* is void because it leads to the alteration of a *Shari'ah* rule.

- *Ibra* during terminal illness in favour of one of the heirs depends on the consent of other heirs, even if the debt is less than one-third of the estate. If *ibra* is made in favour of a stranger, it is considered as *wasiyyah.* It is valid provided it does not exceed one-third of the estate.

> Ibra *is not valid with regard to claims that may come into existence in the future.*

Types of *Ibra*

Ibra can be of two types: specific and general. Specific *ibra* (*ibrakhas*) refers to a type of *ibra* in which a person releases another from a claim arising out of a particular contract such as a claim to recover money arising from the rent or a sale of a specific house. This *ibra* is concerned with a specific right.[3] General *ibra* (*ibra 'aam*), on the other hand, refers to a release from all claims. This may include releasing a person from all claims that might have arisen from different causes, such as the price for a sold item or payment of rent, payment of alimony (*mahr*), or claims arising from deposit.

Ibra can also be classified based on the way the offer is expressed into the following two types: *Bara'at al-isqat,* in which a person releases another by dropping all the rights that he or she has against the person, or by subtracting or diminishing a certain quantity of them.[4] *Bara'atal-istifa* is a type of admission. It is made when a person admits that he or she has received his or her debt or right from another person.

The Effect of an *Ibra*

The effect of an *ibra* is the absolution of a debtor from the liability. The absolution depends on the type of *ibra* that is made. If it is a particular *ibra,* then the debtor is released from a particular debt or claim. However, if it is a general *ibra* in favour of a person, the person is totally released from all claims and debts. It is not allowed for an absolving party to retract his *ibra.* Similarly, it is not valid if a person confesses to a debt from which he is absolved because claims that are waived cannot be revived.

The Differences Between Absolution (*Ibra*) and Gift (*Hibah*)

The following are the differences between the contracts of *ibra and hibah:*

- In *ibra* a debt or a right is waived, whereas in *hibah* a particular thing is given.
- *Ibra* presupposes the existence of a claim between the absolving and the absolved party. In *hibah*, on the other hand, such a pre-existing relationship is not needed.
- In *ibra*, the issue of possession does not arise, whereas a *hibah* contract is not complete unless the receiver obtains possession.

The Contract of Set-Off (*al-Muqassah*)

Literally *muqassah* means equality. Legally, it is defined as a contract in which two debts that are equal in terms of their type, attributes, and settlement dates are set off against each other. It is the cancellation of a creditor's claim on the debtor in lieu of his similar claim on the creditor with certain conditions. When a creditor owes the debtor, set-off may come into operation regarding their mutual debts. In this case, both debts are dropped if they are equal, and the lesser of the two debts is dropped if they are unequal.

Muqasah or the contract of set-off is a method employed for debt-clearance and for the extinction of an obligation. If one of the parties is in breach of contract or defaults in payment, the injured party can, in specified circumstances by way of self-help or set-off, seek redress. The creditor in this case is permitted to appropriate the debtor's property in certain circumstances under the doctrine of *muqasah*. Set-off (*muqasah*), however, is distinguished from a counterclaim. A counterclaim is appropriate in circumstances in which litigation has already commenced in the courts, whereas set-off is extra-indicial and is invoked by a person who objects to bringing legal proceedings. In practice, the right to self-help becomes available automatically on the basis of an existing contract on the occurrence of a given event, for example, retaking of goods or forfeiture of deposit.

Classification of *Muqassah*

Set-off (*muqassah*) is of two types: automatic set-off (*muqassah al-jabriyyah*) and voluntary set-off (*muqassah al-ikhtiariyyah*).

*Automatic Set-Off (*Muqassah al-Jabriyyah*)*

It is an automatic process that comes into operation without the necessity for mutual consent of the two parties. When two parties are indebted to one another at the same time, their debts are annulled by adjustment to the extent of the amount owed by both parties, and the parties are, to that extent, released from their mutual debts. It does not depend on the consent of the parties, nor does it require a demand or request from one of them. For instance, a debtor may sell some of his property to the creditor for immediate payment in the same currency in which he borrowed money or bought a certain property from the creditor. This enables the creditor to claim ownership of the debtor's property to the extent of debtor's indebtedness. In such a situation, automatic set-off happens and, to the majority of the *Fiqh* schools, the consent of the parties is not needed. The Malikii jurists, however, do not agree and argue that set-off should happen by a request from one of the parties and consented by the other.

Conditions for automatic set-off include:

- It can only happen when both parties are creditors and debtors to each other at the same time—for instance, when the purchaser of a certain commodity has a debt on the seller.
- The two debts must be of the same genus, that is, in the same currency, type, and date of maturity. Automatic set-off is not possible when one of the debts is created in gold dinar and the other is in silver dirham or one of the debts is created in Euros and the other in Ringgit or when one of the debts is created in gold dinar and the other in Ringgit. Similarly, the two debts should have the same date of maturity or both should be mature debts. Automatic set-off does not happen when one of the debts is deferred while the other is mature.
- *Muqassah* should not result in any harm to any other person. *Muqassah* is not allowed when one of the debts involves the right of a third person. For instance, when a pledgor sells the pledge property to another creditor, *muqassah* cannot happen because this harms the pledgee who has a priority right on the pledge. Similarly, *muqassah* cannot happen when a bankrupt person sells his property to some of his creditors to the exclusion of others because this may harm other creditors who have equal rights on the same property and are proportionally entitled to have a share in any proceeds from the sale of such properties. However, if a person is not bankrupt, he may sell his properties to one of his creditors. In this case, *muqassah* happens and other creditors cannot object to the sale.
- *Muqassah* should not violate any prohibition imposed by the *Shari'ah*. For example, a person who has bought a certain commodity based on *salam* contract cannot sell it to his creditors prior to obtaining its possession. Similarly, it is not possible for a creditor to enter into a *salam* contract with his debtor using the debt as the price for the *salam* commodity. In a *salam* sale, the price should be present and given during the session of the contract. Thus, a debt cannot become the price for a *salam* commodity.

*Voluntary Set-Off (*Muqassah al-Ikhtiariyyah*)*

Voluntary set-off (*muqassah al-ikhtiaryyah*) refers to a situation in which two debts are created in two different types of currencies. For example, one of the debts could be in gold dinar and the other in silver dirham or one in Ringgit and the other in Euros. If the debts are payable in different currencies—such as one debt is payable in Ringgit and the other in Euros—the parties may enter into *muqassah* contract by mutual consent. For instance, if Ahmad owes Bakar RM 100 and Bakar owes Ahmad Euro 100, muqasahcan still happen. The value of RM 100 in Euros could be set off against Euro 100 and Bakar has to pay the balance in Euros. The exchange rate should be the rate of the day on which the set-off takes place. Voluntary *muqassah* can only happen with the mutual consent of the parties because it will allow them to enter into a set-off at a time when the exchange rate is favourable and acceptable to both of them. Similarly, the mutual consent of the parties is needed when the mode of payment is different. For instance, one debt is paid in instalments, whereas the other is payable instantly, or when one debt is paid in a shorter instalment period and the other debt is paid in a longer instalment period.

Chapter Questions

True/False

1. ( ) The majority of the Muslim jurists argue that the contract of release from liability (*ibra*) is concluded only by an offer.
2. ( ) According to the majority of jurists, an offer of ibra should be immediate and not dependent on a condition.
3. ( ) In a deferred sale contract, if a debtor wants to pay the price in a shorter period the creditor must give him an *ibra.*
4. ( ) It is possible for a person to drop his ownership right over his property through an *ibra.*
5. ( )Absolution (*ibra*) implies both the dropping of a right and its transfer to another person.
6. ( ) It is possible for a person to waive a right that he may acquire in the future.
7. ( ) Set-off or debt clearance (*muqassah*) can happen automatically when the two debts that are equal have different dates of maturity.
8. ( ) A pledgor, by selling the pledged property to the pledgee, can enter into a contract of set-off (*muqassah*) with him.
9. ( ) Set-off or debt clearance (*muqassah*) can happen automatically when the two debts exist simultaneously in two different currencies.
10. ( ) A bankrupt person can sell his or her property to one of his or her creditors and enter into a *muqassah* contract with the creditor.

Short Answer

1. Can a creditor stipulate that the debtor would be released from some of the debt if he settles the balance in a shorter period?
2. Can a debtor claim that the creditor should release him from part of the debt if he settles it in a shorter period?
3. Discuss how the contract of set-off (*muqasah*) could be used in practice as a method to settle debts. Support your answer by providing relevant examples.

4. When Zaki and Kamal were studying overseas, Zaki borrowed from Kamal $1000. Later when both returned to Malaysia, Kamal borrowed RM 2000 from Zaki. Identify the type of *muqassah* contract that they can enter into and the exchange rate that they should agree on.
5. Explain how, in practice, a creditor can enter into a set-off (*muqasah*) contract with his debtor and a pledgee with the pledgor.
6. Define voluntary set-off (*muqasahikhtiyariyah*) and explain why the mutual consent of the parties is needed. Support your answer with relevant examples.

Notes

1. See Wahbah al-Zuhaili, *Financial Transactions in Islamic Jurisprudence*, vol. 2, trans. Mahmoud A. El-Gamal (Beirut: Dar al-Fikr al-Mouaser, 2003), 237–238.
2. See *The Mejelle*, trans C.R. Tyser, D. G. Demetriades, Ismail Haqqi Effendi (Petaling Jaya: The Other Press, 2001), Article 1568.
3. See *The Mejelle*, Article 1537.
4. See *The Mejelle*, Article 1530.

Answers to True/False Questions

Chapter 1: The Contract of Sale (*Bay'*)

1. F
2. F
3. F
4. F
5. T
6. T
7. T
8. T
9. T
10. F
11. F
12. F
13. F
14. T
15. T

Chapter 2: Types and Classifications of Sales

1. F
2. F
3. F
4. T
5. F
6. F
7. T
8. T
9. T
10. F
11. T
12. F
13. F
14. T
15. T

Chapter 3: The Contracts of Employment and Lease (*Ijarah*), Borrowing (*I'arah*), and Reward (*Ja'alah*)

1. F
2. F
3. T
4. F
5. F
6. T
7. T
8. T
9. T
10. F
11. F
12. T

Chapter 4: The Contract of Agency (*Wakalah*)

1. T
2. T
3. T
4. T
5. F
6. T
7. F
8. F
9. T
10. F

Chapter 5: The Contract of Loan (*al-Qard*)

1. F
2. F
3. F
4. F
5. F
6. T
7. T
8. T
9. F
10. T

Chapter 6: The Contract of Safekeeping (*al-Wadi'ah*)

1. F
2. T
3. F

4. F
5. F
6. T
7. T
8. T
9. F
10. T

Chapter 7: Partnership (*al-Sharikat*)

1. F
2. T
3. F
4. F
5. F
6. F
7. F
8. F
9. T
10. F

Chapter 8: Silent Partnership (*Mudarabah/Qirad*)

1. T
2. F
3. F
4. F
5. F
6. F
7. F
8. F
9. F
10. T

Chapter 9: Pledge, Mortgage, or Pawn (*al-Rahn*)

1. T.
2. F
3. T
4. F
5. T
6. T
7. F
8. F
9. T
10. F

Chapter 10: Guarantee (*al-Kafalah*)

1. T.
2. F
3. T
4. T
5. T
6. F
7. T
8. F
9. T
10. F

Chapter 11: Transfer of Debt (*al-Hawalah*)

1. F
2. F
3. T
4. F
5. T

6. F
7. F
8. T
9. T
10. T

Chapter 12: The Contracts of Absolution (*al-Ibra*) and Set-Off (*al-Muqassah*)

1. T
2. T
3. F
4. F
5. T
6. F
7. F
8. T
9. F
10. F

Bibliography

Abu Daud Sulaymanibn al-Ashuath Sijistani. 1990. *Sunan Abu Dawud*. New Delhi: Kitab Bhavan.

Al-Sharanbasi, Ramadhan Ali. 2000. *Al-Nazariyat al-'Aamah fi al-Fiqh al-Islami*. al-Iskandariyyah: Munshaat al-M'arif.

Al-Bahuti, Musa bin Younus. 1402. *Kashaf Al-Qina'*. Beirut: Dar Al-Fikr.

Al-Baihaqi, Ahmad al-Hussain. 1999. *Sunan al-Kubra*. Beirut: Dar al-Kutub al-'Ilmiyah.

Albani, Muhammad Nasir al-Din. 1985. *Irwa al-Galil*. Beirut: Maktabah al-Islami.

Albani, Muhammad Nasir al-Din. 1990. *Da'eef al-Jami' al-Sagheer*. Beirut: Maktabah al-Islami.

Al-Dasuqi, Muhammad bin Ahmad. 2003. *Hashiyah*. Qairo: al-Maktabah al-'Asriyah.

Al-Nawawi, Abu Zakaria. 1992. *Rawdhat al-Talibin*. Beirut: Dar al-Kutub Al-Ilmiyyah.

Al-Qaradawi, Yusuf. 1995. *The Lawful and the Prohibited in Islam*. Trans. Kamal El-Helbawy. Kuala Lumpur: Islamic Book Trust.

Al-Qazwini, Al-Hafiz Abi Abdullah ibn Yazid. 2003. *Sunan Ibn Majah*. Beirut: Dar al-Fikir.

Al-Qurtubi, Muhammad Ibn Ahmad. 1967. *Al-jami' li Ahkam al-Qur'an*. Qairo: Dar al-Kutub.

Al-Sanhuri, 'Abd ar-Razzaq Ahmad. 1997. *Masadir Al-Haqqfil FiqhilIslami*. Qairo: Dar al-Nahdah al-'Arabiyah.

Al-Sherbini, Muhammad bin Ahmad. 2006. *Mughni Al-Muhtaj*. Cairo: Dar al-Hadith.

Al-Shirazi, Abu Ishaq Ibrahim ibn 'Ali. 1995. *Al-Muhadhdhab*. Beirut: Dar al-Kutub al-'lmiyyah.

Al-Zarqa, Mustafa Ahmad. 1999. *Al-Madkhalila Nazriyyat al-Iltizam al-'Aammah fil-Fiqh al islami*. Damascus: Dar al-Qalam.

Al-Zuhaili, Wahbah. 1989. *Al-Fiqh al-Islami Wa Adillatuhu*. Damascus: Dar al-Fikr.

Al-Zuhaili, Wahbah. 2003. *Financial Transactions in Islamic Jurisprudence*. Trans. Mahmoud A. El-Gamal. Beirut: Dar al-Fikr al-Mouaser.

Asad, Muhammad. 1980. *The Message of the Quran*. Gibraltar: Dar al-Andalus.

Fatawa Al Imam Ibn Taimiyya fi Al Muamalat wa Al Ahkam Al Mal. 2005. Cairo: Dar Al Salam. Retrieved from www.dar-alsalam.com.

Ibn 'Abidin, Muhammad 'Amin. 1986. *Hashiyat (Rad al-Mukhtar ala al-Dur al-Mukhtar)*. Makkah al-Mukarramah: Maktabat Makkah al-Mukarramah.

Ibn Hajar, Ahmad ibn 'Ali. 1999. *Fath al-Bari SharhSahih al-Bukhari*. Riyad: Bayt al-Afkar al-Dawliyah.

Ibn Hanbal, Ahmad ibn Muhammad. 1998. *Musnad Ahmad*. Beirut: 'Alam al-Kutub.

Ibn Majah, Muhammad ibn Yazid. 2003. *Sunan ibn Majah*. Delhi: Kitab Bhavan.

Ibn Qudamah, Maufiq al-Din. 2004. *Al-Mughni*. Qairo: Dar al-Hadith.

Ibn Rajab, 'Abd al-Rahman. 1999. *Fath al-Bari SharhSahih al-Bukhari*. Qairo: Dar al-Haramayn.

Ibn Rushd. 2004. *Bidayat al Mujtahid wa Nihayatul Muqtasid*. Qairo: Dar al-'Aqidah.

Islahi, Abdul Azim. 1988. *Economic Concepts of Ibn Taimiyah*. Leicester: The Islamic Foundation.

Kamali, Mohammad Hashim. 2004. *Principles of Islamic Jurisprudence*. (2nd ed.). Kuala Lumpur: Ilmiah Publishers.

Khan, Muhammad Mushin. (1997). *The Translation of the Meaning of Sahih al-Bukhari*. Riyadh: Darussalam.

Malik ibn Anas. 2004. *al-Muwatta*. Trans. Aisha Abdurrahman Bewley. 1997. Spain: Madinah Press Granad.

Mansuri, M. Tahir. 2001. *Islamic Law of Contracts and Business Transactions*. Islamabad: Shari'ah Academy, International Islamic University Islamabad.

The Mejelle, 2001. Trans C.R. Tyser, D. G. Demetriades, Ismail Haqqi Effendi. Petaling Jaya: The Other Press.

Muslim ibn al-Hajjaj al-Qushayri. 2000. *Sahih Muslim*. Beirut: Dar Ihya' al-Turath al-'Arabi.

Obaidullah, Mohammed. 2003. *Islamic Financial Services*. Jeddah: Islamic Economics Research Centre.

The OIC Fiqh Academy, seventh session, item 67/3/7 – no. 4.

Resolutions of the Securities Commission Syariah Advisory Council. 2002. Kuala Lumpur: Securities Commission.

Sabiq, as-Sayyid. 2004. *Fiqh as-Sunnah*. Cairo: Dar al-Hadith.

Saleem, Muhammad Yusuf. 2010. "Methods and Methodologies in Fiqh and Islamic Economics," *Review of Islamic Economics* 14, no. 1: 103–123.

Shariah Standard No. 9, Ijarah and Ijarah Muntahia Bittamleek, AAOIFI: Shariah Standards 1425-6H /2004–2005, 135–158, at 151.

Siddiqui, Abdul Hamid. 1972. *Translation of Sahih Muslim*. Beirut: Dar al-'Arabiyah.

The Holy Qur'an.

Tirmdhi, Muhammad ibn 'Isa. 2000. *Sunan al-Tirmidhi*. Beirut: Dar al-Kutub al-'Ilmiyah.

Usmani, Muhammad Taqi. 2004. *An Introduction to Islamic Finance*. Karachi: Maktaba Ma'ariful Qur'an.

About the Author

Muhammad Yusuf Saleem was born in Afghanistan. He obtained a Bachelor of Laws (LLB) from International Islamic University Malaysia in 1992, where he also studied his Master of Comparative Laws (MCL) and obtained a PhD in 2003. He is currently an Assistant Professor at the Faculty of Economics and Management Sciences, International Islamic University, Malaysia. He has taught a series of courses on *Fiqh* for Economist, Islamic Transactions (*Mu'amalat*), Islamic Jurisprudence (*Usul al-Fiqh*), Islamic banking and finance, *zakat*, *waqf*, and Islamic law of inheritance (*Faraidh*). He has also taught Islamic Finance and *Fiqh al-mu'amalt* courses for post-graduate students at the Graduate School of Management and at the IIUM Institute of Islamic Banking and Finance. Dr. Saleem has contributed several articles to various local and international journals. He has participated and presented papers in international conferences in Kuala Lumpur, Dhaka, Jeddah, and Bahrain. Among his works are *An Introduction to the Theoretical Foundations of Islamic Transactions, Muslim Powerlessness and the Nation-state, Methods and Methodologies in Fiqh and Islamic Economics, Mutawalli Institutions for the Management of Waqf Properties, Form v. Substance in Islamic Banking and Financial Transactions*, and *The Application of Ibra and Muqassah to House Financing Contracts.*

Index

Printed and bound by CPI Group (UK) Ltd, Croydon, CR0 4YY
16/09/2026
02217974-0001